D0886913

THE IMMIGRANT EXPERIENCE

faith, hope, & the golden door

THE IMMIGRANT EXPERIENCE

faith, hope, & the golden door

EDWARD WAKIN

FOREWORD BY THEODORE M. HESBURGH, C.S.C.,
PRESIDENT, UNIVERSITY OF NOTRE DAME

Our Sunday Visitor, Inc.
Huntington, Indiana 46750

ISBN: 0-87973-744-1
Library of Congress Catalog Card Number: 77-78087

Cover Design by Eric Nesheim

Published, printed and bound in the U.S.A. by
Our Sunday Visitor, Inc.
Noll Plaza
Huntington, Indiana 46750

744

*To my Father
and
To my son Daniel*

Books by Edward Wakin

*A Lonely Minority: The Modern Story
        of Egypt's Copts*
The Catholic Campus
*At the Edge of Harlem: Portrait
        of a Middle-Class Negro Family*
*The De-Romanization of the
                American Catholic Church* (with J. F.
        Scheuer)
Controversial Conversations with Catholics
Black Fighting Men in U.S. History
We Were Never Their Age
        (with James DiGiacomo)
The Battle for Childhood
Careers in Communications
Children Without Justice
Enter the Irish-American
Communications: An Introduction to Media
*The Immigrant Experience: Faith, Hope,
        and the Golden Door*

CONTENTS

FOREWORD

In the bicentennial year of 1976, when pessimism about the future of our nation pervaded much commentary, perhaps no subject better illustrated the hope of America than its immigrant experience. During the 1840s and 1850s more than one-fourth of the population of Ireland came to America when a million died in Ireland during the Potato Famine. Before 1890, the largest influx of immigrants was from Germany, Scandinavia, England, and Ireland; afterward it came from Italy, Austria, Hungary, Russia, Poland, and just about everywhere else. In the first two decades of this century, over fourteen and a half million persons passed through Ellis Island, at times at the rate of 8,000 a day, with another 15,000 waiting in New York Harbor. Most were illiterate and possessed only the required twenty-five dollars. All were filled with limitless new hope.

I would like to underline what this meant for America. We have a national motto, in Latin, *e pluribus unum*, on our coins and currency, which says that we are one nation made up of many different people. Have you ever thought of what this really means? We have more black Americans than there are Canadians in Canada, more Spanish-speaking Americans than all the Australians in Australia. Twice as many Jews as there are in Israel. More Indians than when Columbus discovered

America. A quarter of the Irish nation came here after the Potato Famine. There are more Italians by far than the combined populations of Rome, Florence, and Milan, with Naples thrown in. I could say similar things about Germans, Russians, Poles, French, Austrians, Belgians, Greeks, Mexicans, Koreans, Japanese, Chinese, and, most recently, Vietnamese.

Somehow, they all learned to live together, (with increasing comity and tolerance) and, one should add, the kind of virtue that only such an unusual situation could elicit. In a sense, our American/ population, like no other on earth, represents the spread and the variety as well as the yearnings of universal humanity. It was hope that brought so many millions of oppressed, poor, and homeless people to America. Their hopes were mainly realized, even though often with great difficulty. They were our grandparents and great-grandparents. They found freedom and justice here. It was and is the fulfillment of their hopes that gives hope to the world.

We are still a nation of immigrants. About 400,000 new immigrants come into the United States each year legally; more come in illegally. It is estimated that between 4.5 and 8.5 million illegals, mainly from Asia, Africa, the Middle East, Latin America, the Caribbean, and southern Europe, came into the country between 1964 and 1974.

Many observers, including the nation's Catholic bishops, have warned that recent legislation betrays the humanitarianism with which the fortunate should treat the unfortunate. We still have instances of injustice in our immigration laws. Foreign-born persons in the United States are not covered by the Civil Rights Act of 1964, so legal aliens can be discriminated against without recourse. Exclusion grounds remain so severe that a family might not be able to enter the country unless it leaves behind a retarded child. There is no statute of limitations on deportation: someone who was brought in illegally as a child could be deported at retirement. We need a broader legal definition of "refugee" so we can accept more victims of political repression. We need to end the exploitation of illegals, who exist outside the protection of law in employment, housing, education, and medical care. We ought to reconsider our policy of giving special preference to the highly skilled, a policy which often has harmful repercussions in developing countries. We should reinstate preference in other areas by making it easier, for example, for aliens who have children who are U.S. citizens to get visas. We should realize that we are part of the global problems that create immigrants, who are often forced to leave their homes because of insufficient resources and inequitable distribution of the world's goods.

It seems at this writing that President Carter is ready to take the initiative in shaping new immigration policies which reflect the humanitarianism that attracted many people to our country in the first place. This is a welcome development.

America's immigrant experience has made it a microcosm of all the world, with a population that truly represents every nationality, religion, color, and culture on earth. If we can achieve freedom and justice for all here, then maybe there is hope for the rest of the world.

THEODORE M. HESBURGH, C.S.C.
President, University of Notre Dame

1 TO THE GOLDEN DOOR

Praise God!

They had left mothers and fathers weeping at the doorways of huts and hovels. They had picked up a last handful of native soil and felt it go through their fingers like the sands of time. They had turned their backs on the precious land where their sweat had brought forth harvests, leaving behind what was familiar and beloved. They had once been so much at home and then they became strangers. They had uprooted themselves.

They had struggled to ports all over the world, but particularly to those of Europe: Liverpool, Southampton, Bremen, Antwerp, Rotterdam, Le Havre, Glasgow, Piraeus, Fiume, Copenhagen, Constantinople — cities larger than they had ever seen. Finally, after nearly suffocating in steerage, they came into the crowded sunlight to see, as one immigrant recalled, "the beautiful bay and the big woman with the spikes on her head and the lamp that is lighted at night in her hand."

On the pedestal of the Statue of Liberty the famous Emma Lazarus poem was inscribed, setting forth the highest ideals of America's breathtaking invitation to the world:

> Give me your tired, your poor,
> Your huddled masses yearning to breathe free,
> The wretched refuse of your teeming shore,

13

Send these, the homeless tempest-tost to me,
I lift my lamp beside the golden door!

Near the Statue of Liberty on another island — Ellis Island — each immigrant answering the invitation faced the climactic moment. It was an earthly judgment day when they would learn whether they could enter America. After so much they still had to face this. At the Golden Door, the gateway to the promised land for immigrants, where "the streets were paved with gold," they were to discover whether the door would open.

It was that way for 12 to 16 million men, women, and children at Ellis Island, which was established as the gateway to the United States in 1892. No less than one hundred million Americans are linked personally to that dramatic moment of entry by blood relationship to the Ellis Island arrivals.

Once transferred from the ship on which they arrived to a boat or barge, the immigrants were taken to Ellis Island, which became known as the Island of Tears to those turned back — *Tränen Insel* to the Germans, *Isola delle Lagrime* to the Italians. They were taken to the Main Hall, a huge red-brick building with limestone trim and domed towers. Inside, five thousand at a time were crowded into what was the largest room most of the immigrants had ever been in. They filed into a maze of passageways made by metal railings, walking twenty feet apart as U.S. Public Health doctors watched for signs of medical problems.

Chalk marks were used to label those who appeared to need more careful examination: "L" for lameness, "X" for suspected mental defects, "F" for a bad rash on the face. A second doctor looked for specific diseases that were reasons for exclusion, such as tuberculosis and leprosy. A third examined their eyes for symptoms of the blinding disease, trachoma. Where this was suspected, "E" for eyes was chalked onto the immigrant's clothing.

Those with chalk marks were shunted aside for further medical examination, some to be deported. Only about two out of ten actually were detained for more than a few hours at Ellis Island and not more than two out of a hundred actually were sent back. But the arriving strangers knew nothing of the odds in their favor. Each worried about his or her own destiny.

The final test began when the waiting immigrant was summoned from a wooden bench in the giant Registry Hall to appear before an overworked and harried inspector. Looking first at the name tag on the immigrant he then examined the ship's manifest which contained the immigrant's name and twenty-nine pieces of information. With the help of an interpreter, the inspector hurriedly checked the key pieces of information and in less than two minutes made the decision mandated by U.S. law: whether this stranger was "clearly and beyond a doubt entitled to land."

It was almost invariably a quick yes, but that did not lessen the tension. So much was at stake. Bridges had been burned, money scraped together, uprooting completed. For each immigrant it had to be a peak moment, as it was for one elderly Ukrainian farmer. He suddenly bent over the inspector's desk, took his hand, kissed it, and proclaimed, "Praise God!"

Thus the immigrants began the bewildering journey in search of new roots in America, a journey that meant abandoning the familiar and confronting the strange. Their religious faith represented what was familiar. For encountering the strange, they brought hope.

Two dynamic forces came with them through the Golden Door:

Faith. In the Old Country, life was lived in terms of a religious faith that gave meaning to suffering and joy, that was as taken for granted as the breath of daily life. All else had been abandoned, but the immigrants could and did bring their religious faith with them. It therefore became all the more precious. Historian Oscar Handlin emphasizes this commitment in his classic study of immigrants, *The Uprooted*:

15

"These people were anxious that religion do and mean in the United States all that it had back there before the Atlantic crossing. . . . In the American environment, so new and so dangerous, these people felt more need than ever for the support of their faith."

Hope. The immigrants came in order to better themselves and to better the lives of their children. On this hope was built the history of "A Nation of Immigrants" (as President John F. Kennedy called the United States).

To understand America is to know of the faith and the hope that vitalized the lives of its immigrants. "It is necessary," President Kennedy pointed out, "to know why over 42 million people gave up their settled lives to start anew in a strange land. We must know how they met the new land and how it met them, and, most important, we must know what these things mean for our present and for our future."

For President Kennedy, the immigrant line stretched back only two generations — to an immigrant saloonkeeper in Boston. He was a third-generation American, whereas President Franklin D. Roosevelt could recall to the Daughters of the American Revolution in 1938 that his ancestors went back to the *Mayflower*. Still, President Roosevelt reminded the DAR, they were immigrants, all of them: "Remember, remember always that all of us, and you and I especially, are descended from immigrants and revolutionists."

The historic significance of immigration was summed up by President Harry Truman's Commission on Immigration and Naturalization in 1953. "Our growth as a nation has been achieved, in large measure, through the genius and industry of immigrants of every race and from every quarter of the world," it stated. "The story of their pursuit of happiness is the saga of America. Their brains and their brawn helped to settle our land, to advance our agriculture, to build our industries, to develop our commerce, to produce new inventions and, in general, to make us the leading nation that we now are."

Between 1800 and 1914, thirty-five million immigrants came to the United States. The five million who came between 1815 and 1860 were more than the entire population of the United States when the first census was taken in 1790. In a single decade, 1845-54, three million immigrants arrived in a country of only twenty million, which meant that in only one ten-year period three Americans out of every twenty had recently arrived.

In proportion to the size of the population, that was the heaviest influx of immigrants, but for sheer numbers nothing surpassed the early part of this century. In the peak decade between 1904 and 1914 a total of ten million arrived. In 1907, the biggest year, there were more than 1.25 million. On a single record-breaking day in that year, April 17, the United States admitted 11,745 immigrants.

The overwhelming majority came from Europe. First from the British Isles, particularly Ireland. Then came the great tides from western Europe and Scandinavia, followed by those from the Mediterranean and Slavic countries. When the immigrant totals were sorted out for the century and a half from 1800 to 1950, eighty-five percent of the immigrants had come from Europe. Eleven percent had come from other countries in the American Hemisphere and the remainder from the rest of the world.

Nineteenth-century immigration to the United States was called one of the wonders of the age. Nothing had compared with it "since the encampments of the Roman Empire or the tents of the crusaders." In country after country, the desire to emigrate resembled an emotional epidemic. It was spread by books about America, by descriptions in popular newspapers, and, particularly, by enthusiastic letters sent home by immigrants.

As the British *Spectator* noted in 1851 about the continuing high tide of Irish emigration, "a large amount of printed matter about America" appealed to the greater numbers who were learning to read, but "this influence is trifling when compared with that of private letters from America." In 1864, an official U.S. report pointed out that very little was done by the government to encourage a "purely voluntary" exodus from Europe, "induced by letters from their friends in this country advising them to join them here."

The overall reason for emigration to the United States resulted from a basic human response: things were worse in the Old Country, better in the New World. As the population of Europe was doubling in the century after 1750, opportunities were shrinking for large masses of people. The poor were getting poorer and even those who owned meager plots of land were finding it harder to eke out an existence. Changes in farming and labor conditions made matters worse rather than better. And in one country or another at various times religious and political discontent added to the immigration "epidemic."

Meanwhile, the American dream beckoned, as did the shipping companies that brought freight to Europe in the booming transatlantic traffic. What shippers wanted and promoted was a special kind of cargo for the return trip — immigrants. Early in the nineteenth century, the American consul in Dublin was already reporting that "the principal freight from Ireland to the United States consists of passengers." Then, in the 1860s when steamships took over from sailing ships, transatlantic travel became faster, easier, and safer.

A push-pull rhythm was at work. Conditions at home *pushed* immigrants to leave; conditions in America *pulled* them across the waters. As became evident every time the U.S. economy declined, the pull was stronger than the push. When opportunities slumped in America, the word got back and emigration slumped too.

Overall, the tide of immigration was divided into the "old" and the "new." Until the 1890s, the immigrant movement came largely from northern and western Europe. It was dominated by the Irish, the Germans, and the Scandinavians and known as the "old" immigration. Then, the tide shifted to southern and eastern Europe, with Italians, Poles, and Jews predominating. Whereas in 1882, eighty-seven percent of the immigrants came from northern and western Europe, in the peak immigration year of 1907 eighty-one percent came from southern and eastern Europe.

This was dramatized at Ellis Island where the "new" immigrants were processed by the "old" immigrants — who had so much trouble spelling their names. Closed in 1954, Ellis Island appropriately was reopened for visits beginning with the U.S. bicentennial year. The reopening ceremonies were an occasion for emotional reminiscences for returning immigrants, such as Anthony De Gennaro. Sixty-four years before, he had arrived with his father as a frightened youngster clutching a passport from Regia d'Italia. "We did not know any English," he recalled. "We were terribly frightened. We thought: what if some of us are admitted and the others do not pass the examination?"

The De Gennaro father-and-son story after Ellis Island typifies the unwritten rule of American history during the decades of immigration. The father bettered himself by leaving the Old Country; the son was expected to do better than the father — and he almost invariably did. De Gennaro senior became a longshoreman and then bought a grocery store; his son became a mechanical engineer and retired after thirty-eight years as an executive at the American Can Company.

With each immigrant group, this story of hope realized was played out, a collection of individual dramas and a collective ethnic drama. Each group lived out a distinctive American odyssey, side by side with all the other immigrant groups. In chronicling the American experience of major immigrant groups — Irish, Germans, Scandinavians, Italians, Poles, Jews, and many others — it is clear that they were merged into American life, but *not* melted down — contrary to predictions.

Only six years after the birth of the United States, Jean de Crèvecoeur set down his frequently quoted prediction that people from all over the world would be "melted into a new race of men." The phrase *melting pot* was taken for granted as a

19

description of what was happening in the United States when the country cheered a 1908 hit play called *The Melting Pot*. The leading character, an immigrant, announced that the "real American . . . will be the fusion of all the races, the coming superman."

But even the play's author, Israel Zangwill, later dismissed this view of America, for "nature will return even if driven out with a pitchfork." For it was the nature of the different immigrant groups to experience America in terms of who they were and where they came from and each wrote its own biography — different and also similar. *Different* because each was different to start with and this shaped their American experience, with colorful, touching, remarkable, enriching differences that help to explain America as well as the country's ethnic riches. *Similar* because after going through the Golden Door each immigrant group acted out its own version of the dynamic forces of faith and hope.

2 THE IRISH

*But ivrybody is an
Irishman on Pathrick's Day*

*Whin we luck at him there, we see our blissed Saviour,
stripped a'most naked lake ourselves; whin we luck at
the crown i'thorns on the head, we see them mockin'
him, just the same as — some people mock ourselves for
our religion; whin we luck at his eyes, we see they wor
niver dry, like our own; whin we luck at the wound in his
side, why we think less of our own wounds an' bruises,
we get 'ithin and 'ithout, every day av our lives.*

    Thus did one Kathleen Kennedy of Boston describe in 1848
what it was like to be Irish, Catholic, and an immigrant newly
come to the shores of America; poor, unlettered, unskilled,
and victimized. The Irish, arriving in sudden and large
numbers during the 1840s as the first major wave of immigrants, found themselves disdained for their religion, despised for their poverty, and depicted as "brutal, base, cruel
cowards, and as insolent as base" (in the scathing comment of
a prominent New Yorker).
    Fleeing the catastrophic Irish Famine of the late 1840s,
they arrived with high hopes and little else. They landed mainly in New York or Boston and huddled together there or in

other American cities, where they had to depend on hard labor and their own kind to make their way. That they succeeded so dramatically tends to blur the tremendous leap forward from the unknown Kathleen Kennedy of 1848 to the famous Kennedys of some one hundred years later, the leap from persecuted members of a beleaguered immigrant Church to proud adherents of the largest religious organization in America, from despised newcomers to political leaders.

The Irish transformed their position in America by a combination of piety, politics, and patriotism, symbolized by the fourth "P" represented by St. Patrick's Day and energized by their militancy. They shaped and dramatized the immigrant experience for all the nationalities that followed them to America, demonstrating that immigrants could be both American and Irish (or German, Polish, Italian, or whatever). At the same time, they loved the old country and were devoted to the new one. They were loudly and proudly Irish — and American, too.

Irish success in winning acceptance for their double identity is symbolized in St. Patrick's Day. It became a day not only for the Irish but also for nearly everyone else. As early as 1852, one impressed bystander at New York's first giant St. Patrick's Day parade blurted out in admiration: "Why, sure these can't be all Irish!" Or, as the irrepressible Irish-American humorist Finley Peter Dunne had his celebrated character "Mr. Dooley" observe: "But ivrybody is an Irishman on Pathrick's Day."

Above all, Irish-Americans have been devoted to the Roman Catholic Church. They led the way in building and filling its churches and schools, in contributing its priests and particularly its bishops, and in merging ethnic and religious identity. Historian George Potter has rightly called the American Catholic Church their "greatest collective achievement."

An Irish priest in upstate New York, Father P. J. M. Reilly, depicted the typical religious commitment of his countrymen and women when he wrote in the 1830s of the "zeal which I saw the poor creatures manifest in attendance in the services of their religion." They entered his "temporary little place of worship" from homes beyond the Catskills "on the morning of Sunday, pale, wayworn, and fasting, having travelled all the night of Saturday." Father Reilly resolved to build "a church which would be to them a bond of union, and a resting place, around whose walls they might deposit in sacred security the mortal remains of their kindred, with the deep, enduring affection of Ireland, which buries its heart in the 'grave with those it loves.' "

For newly-arrived Irish, their faith was their bond in this world as well as their guarantor of reward in the next. It was the source of their identity and the fountainhead of their certainties. The Church was the one place in America where they had no doubt that they belonged and where no one else had any doubt either. Even before the massive arrival of the Irish, Patrick S. Casserly, an Irish-American schoolmaster and essayist, pointed out: "In this country, the idea of Catholicity and Ireland is so blended in the minds of the American people, as to be in a manner inseparable."

The American impression matched the Irish intention. The Irish were militant in defending their Catholicism and they played a major role in the incredible expansion of the Catholic Church in America. They added zeal to their growing numbers in a country where less than one in a hundred had been Catholic in the original Thirteen Colonies.

Irish-Americans swelled the membership of their Church. Between 1846 and 1851 more than 870,000 Irish went to America; by 1860, more than 1.6 million lived in the United States. Meanwhile, between 1840 and 1880, the number of American Catholics increased tenfold, from 600,000 to over six million. By the turn of this century, one in six Americans was a Catholic.

As James Cardinal Gibbons, who became the acknowledged leader of the American Catholic Church, said in (appropriately) an 1871 St. Patrick's Day sermon: "Is not this country chiefly indebted to her [Ireland] for its faith? There are few churches erected from Maine to California, from Canada to Mexico, which Irish hands have not helped to build, which Irish purses have not supported, and in which Irish hearts are not found worshipping. She contributes not only to the *materiel* but also to the *personnel* of the Church in this country. A large proportion of our Bishops and clergy are of Irish origin or descent." Another leading figure in the U.S. Church, Bishop John L. Lancaster Spalding, summed up the Irish contribution late in the nineteenth century: "No other people could have done for the Catholic faith in the United States what the Irish people have done."

Although the Irish were not the only immigrant group that provided large numbers of Catholics, as the first large influx they inevitably predominated. Between 1789 and 1935, 268 of 464 U.S. bishops were born in Ireland or were the sons of Irish immigrants. (This does not include third-generation Irish bishops.) In 1886, of the 69 bishops in the United States 35 were Irish; the Germans came second with only 15. "The Germans are a pillar of the Church in America, but the Irish have always held the rooftop," Sir Shane Leslie noted in the *Dublin Review* of August 1918.

In politics, the Irish demonstrated a similar capacity to gain power, and, in fact, shaped the political life of American cities in the process of predominating in the Democratic Party. "Irish" implied Democrat as well as Catholic. "Here comes a shipload of Irish," the English poet Charles Latrobe wrote as early as the 1830s. "They land upon the wharfs of New York in rags and one-knee'd breeches, with raw looks and bare necks. They flourish their cudgels, throw up their town hats, and cry, 'Hurrah for Gineral Jackson.' "

The Irish made ethnic voting a major factor on Election Day. Recognizing that the Irish were clustered in the cities where their vote was of primary importance, politicians went all-out to attract their support. Indeed, what now is regarded as a patronizing remark was used as far back as 1832 when

Henry Clay, running for president on the Whig ticket, told a St. Patrick's Day dinner: "Some of my nearest and dearest friends [are] Irishmen."

In 1884, one of the biggest political blunders in American history cost the Republican presidential candidate the election by offending the Irish vote. It happened on the steps of New York's Fifth Avenue Hotel when a Protestant clergyman spewed out anti-Irish, anti-Catholic sentiments typical of the time. In greeting the Republican candidate, James G. Blaine, he blustered: "We are Republicans, and don't propose to leave our party, and identify ourselves with the party whose antecedents have been RUM, ROMANISM, AND REBELLION."

That did it. The Republicans had been making headway with the Irish vote against the Democratic candidate, Grover Cleveland, and Blaine had come to town to close his campaign. Then up came the provocative reference to Irish drinking, faith, and Old Country politics and down went the Irish support for Blaine. Cleveland carried New York State by a mere 1,149 votes out of 1.67 million cast and everyone agreed that the widely-publicized slur cost Blaine much more than that in Irish votes. The loss of New York cost Blaine the election and Cleveland became the first Democrat to be elected president after the Civil War.

In politics, the Irish had numbers on their side as well as strong loyalties. They could be counted on to turn out for election days as well as holy days. Militant and determined, they shaped and came to dominate the political machines in America's rapidly-growing cities. From Chicago's Michael ("Hinky Dink") Kenna to Boston's John ("Honey Fitz") Fitzgerald, from San Francisco's Christopher A. Buckley to New York's "Honest John" Kelly, the epitome of a political boss was a cigar-smoking Irishman. They were smart, ambitious men who reached for the big brass rings of success in one of the few areas where opportunity was available to a poor, uneducated Irish lad who was looked down upon by established Protestant Americans.

In Church and politics, the Irish displayed a remarkable talent for organization, much-needed in a time of chaotic expansion and growth in industrializing and urbanizing America. New York's "Honest John" Kelly is an example. As one historian has noted, Kelly demonstrated the "same genius for organization which made the Irish so successful as leaders in the Church." An admirer observed that Kelly found the New York machine (originally dominated by Protestants who excluded the Irish) "a horde" and left it "an army."

What the political machines provided was what all immigrants needed: a haven in the cold, uninviting atmosphere of the American city. The Irish turned to their priests and politicians, as would later immigrant groups, but they seemed to do it with more intensity than any others. It made sense after all: they needed all the assistance they could get in a dog-eat-dog society where government did not offer a helping hand. So they resorted to their priests (who in Ireland had always been very close to the people and shared the common lot of British persecution) and to their own kind as politicians.

When the famous muckraker Lincoln Steffens asked the boss of Boston, Martin Lomasney, about the role of political machines, he received a straight no-nonsense response. It echoes with the hardships of tenement life, hunting for jobs, and making ends meet: "I think there's got to be in every ward somebody that any bloke can come to — no matter what he's done — and get help. Help, you understand; none of your law and your justice, but help."

Political machines provided direct, uninhibited assistance of the kind one neighbor would give another in Ireland. It was the source of their political power, as explained by one of the most colorful Tammany Hall figures, George Washington Plunkitt. "If a family is burned out," Plunkitt explained, "I don't ask whether they are Republicans or Democrats, and I don't refer them to the Charity Organization Service which would investigate their case in a month or two and decide they were worthy of help about the time they are dead from starvation. I just get quarters for them, buy clothes for them if their clothes were burned up, and fix them up till they got things runnin' again. It's philanthropy but it's politics — mighty good politics. Who can tell how many votes one of these fires bring me?"

The Irish also faced widespread bigotry in addition to a lack of skills. As stated in an official New York report in 1870, "unfortunately, they [the Irish] are mostly rude uninstructed laborers of the lowest grade." The jobs they did get were mainly of the backbreaking kind: carters, porters, street cleaners, hod carriers, stevedores, construction men, canal and railroad workers. They also filled many of the waiters' jobs. The women became much-desired servants in the homes of the well-to-do, once a pressing need for domestics overcame anti-Irish bias. (An 1853 ad in the *New York Daily Sun* read: "Woman wanted — To do general housework . . . English, Scotch, Welsh . . . or any country or color except Irish.")

For the Irish, who were primarily country folk, the city became a new and often demoralizing environment. Yet, that is what the Irish became in America: city dwellers. They stayed in the cities because they usually did not have enough money to travel any farther than their port of entry, because their experiences with famine and rural poverty in Ireland made them suspicious of the land, and because they found it most attractive to stay among their own kind. As one observer noted, Irish immigrants "rejected the land, for the land had rejected them."

As particularly fraternal people, the Irish shuddered at the thought of the wide-open spaces of the American West. And, for that matter, they had had little chance in the Old Country to develop the skills and aptitude for frontier farming. In the cities, they were among their own kind to pray, to parade, and to have a drink in the neighborhood saloon. Like the pub in Ireland, the saloon was the social center where a poor Irishman could go, be among friends, get advice, borrow money, and not feel all alone.

Sociability was the hallmark of country life in Ireland and an Irishman living on an isolated American farm missed it sorely. One such immigrant in Missouri wrote home nostalgically: "I could then go to a fair or a wake, or dance. . . . I could spend the winter nights in a neighbour's house cracking jokes by the turf fire. If I had there but a sore head I could have a neighbour within every hundred yards of me that would run to see me. But here everyone can get so much land, and generally has so much, that they calls them neighbours that live two or three miles off — och! the sorra take such neighbours, that made me leave home."

Attempts were made to urge the Irish to homestead and farm, but to no avail. In 1880, for instance, the U.S. Census reported that almost half of the foreign-born Irish were living in only four cities: New York, Philadelphia, Brooklyn (then a separate city), and Boston. In the cities where they lived, they enthusiastically banded together in social clubs, militia companies, firefighting brigades, literary groups, and charitable societies. They loved a parade and delighted in donning uniforms to march up Main Street with the Emmett Guards or the Mitchel Light Guard (in New York), the Hibernia Guards (in Philadephia), the Montgomery Guards, the Columbia Artillery, or the Sarsfield Guards (in Boston).

When they expressed their patriotism as Americans, the Irish joined to form Irish units and went to war carrying the symbols of Erin. Along with the Stars and Stripes, they waved green banners displaying the Irish harp, a sunburst, shamrocks, and Gaelic slogans. With the coming of the Civil War, the same Irishmen who had been disdained as rowdies were urged even in chilly New England to help save the Union. Recruiting ads urged: "You have fought nobly for the Harp and Shamrock. Fight now for the Stars and Stripes. . . . Your adopted country wants you."

For the Irish, the Civil War became a milestone in winning acceptance in America. Until then, they had been on the defensive in the face of anti-Catholic, anti-Irish campaigns and riots. In the 1830s, an observer remarked that publication of anti-Catholic books had become "a part of the regular industry of the country, as much as the making of nutmegs or the construction of clocks."

The most infamous example was a literary hoax titled *Awful Disclosures of Maria Monk,* an 1836 book filled with fictional scandal about life in a nunnery. It was written by a ghost-writer and attributed to one Maria Monk, supposedly a former nun. Actually, she had never been in a convent and was only a front for the ravings of a Canadian minister. Nonetheless, the appetite for anti-Catholic literature was such that the book went through twenty printings and sold three hundred thousand copies prior to the Civil War.

Meanwhile, the infamous Know-Nothing Party had been formed in 1849. It was the most prominent of the various anti-Catholic organizations that were appearing throughout America. Their members were committed to opposing Catholics and favoring only "American-born" for political office. The Irish felt the brunt on two counts: Irish and Catholic were considered synonymous, and the Irish themselves constituted forty-three percent of the foreign-born population by 1850 (twice the proportion of the next largest group, the Germans).

When the Union turned to the Irish at the outbreak of the Civil War in 1861, the Irish military hero Thomas Francis Meagher could proclaim in Boston, the city that had been toughest on the Sons of Erin: "Here at this hour I proclaim it . . . Know-Nothingism is dead. This war, if it brought no other excellent and salutary fruits, brought with it this result, that the Irish soldier will henceforth take his stand proudly by the side of the native-born, and will not fear to look him straight and sternly in the face, and tell him that he has been equal to him in his allegiance to the Constitution."

Before the Civil War, the phrase "fighting Irish" conjured popular visions of rowdy, riotous, tipsy Paddys who were "sociable with paving blocks" and who "get drunk, meet their friend, and for love knock him down." During the Civil War, the phrase was capitalized and transformed. "Fighting Irish" became a proud, heroic label as green banners were covered with red blood on the battlefields of the Civil War.

The Irish 69th Regiment became the famous "Fighting 69th," mobilized only eleven days after the firing on Fort Sumter. The press glamorized it and other Irish units throughout the Civil War, celebrating their heroics. As one war correspondent reported after the first Battle of Bull Run, "strolling, drunken vagabonds . . . picked up in the low groggeries" of New York "fought like tigers."

Although the Irish had no particular enthusiasm for the abolition of slavery, they rallied behind the Union struggle to save the Republic. As the Boston *Pilot* thundered on behalf of its faithful Irish readers: "The Union — It Must Be Preserved! The *Pilot* Knows No North, No South." The fate of the United States, which had become the home of their "exile" from Ireland, was at stake and the Irish responded in numbers greater than their proportion of the population. Official figures listed 144,221 Irish-born soldiers and officers, but estimates run higher, to more than double that total.

On the battlefield, the Irish mixed their piety with their patriotism. Both traits made an impact upon the American public as the press reported on the Irish in action and at prayer. One moment, according to a contemporary account, Irish soldiers "knelt down to receive, bare-headed, the benediction of their priest, next moment rushed into the fray with a wilder cheer and a more impetuous dash." A "distinguished colonel of genuine American race" told the visiting Irish writer John Francis Maguire: "Why sir, if I wanted to storm the gates of hell, I didn't want any finer or braver fellows than those Irishmen. . . . I saw them in battle, sir; but I also saw them sick and dying in the hospital, and how their religion gave them courage to meet death with cheerful resignation."

Unlike any previous event in U.S. history, the Civil War brought together immigrants and native-born Americans in a joint enterprise. The social and psychological chasm of the cities was bridged as men fought and died together and as immigrants played a prominent role in saving the Republic. Most prominent in this effort were the two largest immigrant groups of that period, the Irish and the Germans.

Along with their devotion to their adopted country, the Irish also were locked into powerful love-hate emotions — love for the Old Country and hatred for its oppressor, Great Britain. Wherever Maguire traveled in post-Civil War America, he found "the same feeling of passionate love, the same feeling of passionate hate" among the Irish. As far back as 1842, as their numbers started to swell, Irish-Americans had held a national gathering on behalf of Ireland.

The Irish blamed the British for conditions in Ireland and they had both personal experiences and well-remembered history to fuel their emotions. Beginning with twelfth-century incursions, the English had been determined to bring the Irish to heel — and the Irish just as determined to resist them. Persistently rebellious, they periodically rose against their English overlords and each time suffered for it. The English imposed the infamous Penal Laws, whose spirit was summed up by Lord Chancellor Bowen: "The law does not suppose any such person to exist as an Irish Roman Catholic." After the victory of William of Orange at the Battle of the Boyne in 1690, the Penal Laws were carried to devastating extremes and the target was clear: Irish Catholics.

The four out of five Irish who were Catholics could not vote, sit in Parliament, serve on a jury, teach school, enter a university, work for the government, manufacture or sell books, or carry a gun. Catholic priests had to register their names and parishes under penalty of branding and were confined to the boundaries of those parishes. Catholic churches could not have belfries, towers, or steeples. These laws, which survived in one form or another into the twentieth century, were burned into the memories of Irish immigrants, the overwhelming majority of whom were Catholics. During the peak years of post-famine migration, almost half of all Irish im-

31

migrants were coming from six of Ireland's thirty-two counties: Cork, Kerry, Tipperary, Limerick, Galway, and Mayo.

England's handling of the Irish Famine turned hostility into irrevocable hatred and left the immigrants eager and ready to support any campaigns that were anti-English and/or pro-Irish independence. No effort became more celebrated than that of the Fenians, the revolutionary movement mobilized in post-Civil War America to free Ireland. The Fenians were an outlet for the volatile Irish love-hate feelings, which were epitomized in an experience described by an Irish priest who had pleaded with a devoted immigrant father of seven to return to the sacraments. The father's problem was the matter of forgiving the English for what they had done in Ireland. When he told the priest why he hated the English, his religious piety and his painful memories collided head-on.

As reported by the visiting journalist John Francis Maguire, the man told the priest that "still there's something in me that I can't get over. . . . I told your reverence I was turned out of my land, where my father and his people before him lived. I don't know how long. . . . There didn't come out of the heavens a bitterer morning when the sheriff was at my door with the crowbar men, and a power of peelers, and the army too, as if 'twas going to war they were, instead of coming to drive an honest man and his family from house and home."

Because of the cold, his father died the same night under a shelter made for him with a few sticks and a quilt. His wife died the next day after giving birth to a baby girl in a ditch. "I know my religion well enough to tell me I must forgive my enemies, or I can't get absolution," he told the priest. Yet, he could not forgive and forget. "I'll never forgive the bloody English government that allowed a man to be treated worse than I'd treat a dog, let alone a Christian, and sent their peelers and their army to help them to do it to me and others."

Finally, an illness of the daughter born after the eviction "softened the father's heart" and he uttered the word "forgiveness." But he did not forget. And, as Maguire reported,

Irishmen like him were scattered throughout the United States as "willing contributors to Fenian funds, and enthusiastic supporters of anti-British organizations."

So Irish immigrants cheered in 1865 when the Fenians held a national convention in Philadelphia and drafted a constitution providing for a president and a congress. It was an incredible event in immigrant history: Irishmen were setting up their own state within a state. At the Fenians' New York City headquarters in a Union Square mansion, their flag of harp and sunburst flew boldly. They then set in motion a plan that was noted more for its daring than for its wisdom, more for its presumption than for its practicality. It was an invasion of Canada, which they hoped would start a chain reaction that would lead to revolution in Ireland and Canada. Or, if not that, to the exchange of a Fenian-conquered Canada for an Ireland freed of British rule.

The Fenian Secretary of War, General T. W. Sweeny (a hero of the Mexican War and a Civil War infantry commander), mapped a three-pronged invasion of Canada, with the main force coming from Buffalo. During May 1866, Fenians poured into Buffalo from all over the country and actually invaded Canada on the night of May 31. They managed to capture the village of Fort Erie before giving up and returning to Buffalo three days later.

The audacious failure did succeed, however, in mobilizing Irish-American emotions and demonstrating how strongly the immigrants felt their love of Ireland and hatred of Britain. Today, on the side of a seafood restaurant in Buffalo, a plaque commemorates those strong feelings and that bizarre invasion: "In this vicinity, from the dock of the Pratt Iron Works, on the night of May 31, 1866, the Fenians embarked for Canada in the cause of independence for Ireland." The plaque had been set in place one hundred years later.

During the same period, Irish militancy was being directed against the domestic tyranny appearing in the form of inhuman conditions in the Pennsylvania coal mines. There, retribu-

33

tion was in the form of underground terrorism by the Molly Maguires against mine operators and bosses, culminating in nine murders during 1874-75. Ironically, the mine owners were led by an Irishman, Franklin B. Gowen, who hired another Irishman, James McParlan, to infiltrate and expose the Molly Maguires. With the help of high-handed legal proceedings, nineteen Molly Maguires were tried and then hung in 1876, leaving resentment and bitterness. The incident provided yet another reminder that the Irish, more than any other immigrant group, were ready to strike back.

By the end of the nineteenth century, the Irish mystique had spread throughout America. Hard-working and tough-minded, the Irish did nothing in halves, whether fighting for America or against England, whether going to church or going to vote, whether complaining or celebrating. They were unsurpassedly militant. And they had no intention of letting anyone forget that being Irish was a special thing to be.

America came to believe them, too. By the time of the Spanish-American War and the U.S. victory at San Juan Hill, war correspondents raced around looking for the first soldier to reach the top, assuming that it would be a "red-haired Irishman." They were disappointed to find it was a German-American. When the American Expeditionary Force went into battle for the first time in World War I, correspondents went looking for that same "red-haired Irishman."

In describing the way men rushed to volunteer for the "Fighting 69th" Regiment when the United States entered World War I, its famous chaplain, Father Francis Patrick Duffy, pointed out that it was not only the Irish who wanted to join up. He observed that a number of the "Irish" volunteers "bore distinctly German, French, Italian, or Polish names." They were "Irish by adoption, Irish by association, or Irish by conviction." Whatever they were, they were eager to join up with the "Fighting Irish" of the 69th Regiment and to share the Irish pride in being Irish.

It all comes together in St. Patrick's Day: that pride in

ethnic identity which other ethnic groups reinvigorated in the 1960s and 1970s. The Irish started celebrating the day as early as 1737 and by the time of the American Revolution it was "enthusiastically observed in the American army," reports one chronicler. The banquets that hailed St. Patrick could no longer handle all the celebrants and yielded first place to the now-familiar parades.

Everyone cheered the St. Patrick's Day parade, including those bellwethers of public feelings, the press and the politicians. In New York's 1870 parade, the mayor (not an Irishman) not only wore a shamrock but displayed a green tie, green gloves, and a green coat. *The New York Times* editorial cheer was typical: "Let us think of the procession and the pageant, of the harp and the sunburst, of the cheerful lads and blushing lasses and of the rich brogue." The parade itself was described as "full of heart and soul . . . all compact of significance and enthusiasm — an outpouring of genuine rejoicing, a boiling over, in a word, of jovial patriotism and effervescent vitality."

In all this celebration of the Irish in America and of their pride in identity, the final words surely belong to such as the *Irish World* when, in 1892, it answered the question, "How Long Will St. Patrick's Day Live Among Irish-Americans?"

> While in veins of Irish manhood flows one drop of Irish blood;
> While in hearts of Ireland's daughters beats true Irish womanhood;
> While God sends to Irish mothers babes to suckle, boys to rear;
> While God sends to Irish fathers one man child thy name to bear.

3 THE GERMANS

Fewer big prizes,
but also fewer blanks

*As far as I, myself, am concerned, laying my hand on
my heart, I cannot say otherwise than that I thank God
that I am here; that I only regret not having come
sooner.*

Writing home to Elberfeld, Germany, in the middle of the
nineteenth century, a farmer named Johann Friedrich Diederich described his new life in America. He was settled with
his family at Manitouwoc Rapids on Lake Michigan, living an
immigrant life which was a mixture of hard work, fertile land,
Bible reading, and an outlook for "a pleasant life and a safe future."

Wherever they went in America, the Germans stood out as
newcomers who would, in the current phrase, "hang in there."
They would abide and they would overcome through a combination of persistence and hard work. That became the external
sign of their equation of faith and hope. Industrious rather than
adventuresome, eager to dig in and settle down rather than to
wander around and speculate on land holdings, they sowed
prudently, harvested earnestly, and prayed devoutly.

One German traveling in the United States reported in

1846: "On the whole the German settlers are highly commended as industrious, moral, persevering, and adverse to novelty and change." Or, as one historian of immigration said of the German's pursuit of the American dream, he took "fewer chances in the lottery of life than his enterprising Scotch-Irish or limber-minded Yankee neighbor." He drew from life "fewer big prizes, but also fewer blanks."

A day in the mid-nineteenth-century life of the Diederich family (father, mother, and four children) reflects that mixture of hard work and faith. Luckier than most immigrants, they had arrived with enough money to buy "80 acres of rolling country, facing east, forested, with a small brook and meadow," ninety miles east of Milwaukee.

Johann Diederich described getting up with the sun at 6:00 or 6:30 A.M., reading "God's word together," and drinking coffee. Everyone went to work immediately after breakfast and stopped only for a noon lunch of white beans and bacon or dumpling with bacon. As soon as lunch was over, they went back to work until it was too dark to work any longer. Then came dinner: "Having fed ourselves, we read a chapter from the Bible together and then we gather around the warm stove" to talk of relatives and friends in the Old Country. He added: "Usually, however, I am so tired out from the day's hard labors that I am too exhausted even to smoke a pipe."

Nonetheless, having come to America, Johann Diederich wrote to his relatives: "Yes, things are really good here, for people who have money but also for people who have none, provided the latter are industrious, diligent workers or artisans. . . . The immigrant, especially the man who has no money, must be self-reliant and he cannot be lacking in endurance."

Although working hard may have been second nature to German immigrants, it was not always applauded by native Americans. Like others, they suffered because of the strangeness of their language, dress, and manner. In the Midwest, for instance, the prudent, conservative German farmer looked different to resentful American neighbors who tended to see him as penny-pinching, frugal, and materialistic.

Writing home, a German farmer in Missouri described the situation as he saw it: "There is scarcely a farm that is not for sale, for the American farmer has no love for home, such as the German has. I am building a smokehouse, a kitchen, a milk-house over one of the excellent springs near our house, a stable for the horses and one for the cows. My American neighbors say that I am building a town. . . ." In German eyes, American neighbors sat around the fireplace all day, whittling and "spitting into the fire" or they went out visiting and hunting while their farms went to seed.

In the cities, where Germans were just as likely to settle as on the farms, they were quick to go to work. Again, it was not to applause. One 1850 guidebook for immigrants complained that a newly-arrived German in Buffalo "who was unable to speak a word of English, took a job of chopping firewood out of a Yankee's hands." It then admitted grudgingly of immigrant Germans: "They are very industrious people; they hoard up their money, get all their paper money converted into hard cash, and send their children about to the boardinghouses to beg the scraps of offal meat. They are utterly disliked by the laboring Yankees, and, indeed, by all except those who employ them; yet they are, notwithstanding, truly faithful and honest in their transactions."

Faced with hostility from native Americans, the Germans stood even firmer in their commitment to fraternal and benevolent societies, to their parochial schools, and to their churches. In the period before the American Civil War, Catholic Germans organized many colonization projects, short-lived groups which fought the wilderness rather than face religious and ethnic prejudice in the cities.

The Hungarian-born superior of the Redemptorists in the United States, Father Alexander Czvitkovicz, reported on a field trip to help one such group in the forests of northeastern Pennsylvania. In 1843, he wrote about the grinding effort of converting forest to farmland: "One meets at almost every step thick brushwood, roots intertwined with the branches which bend to the ground, entire trees uprooted by age and the winds, heaped up here and there like impassable ramparts; moreover, since the sun is not able to penetrate beneath these vaults of foliage it is very humid, the ground is so slippery that one is never sure of his footing and has almost as many falls as steps."

Those Germans who arrived in the first half of the nineteenth century became known as the "Grays" — solid, steadfast, stable peasants who came from hard-pressed rural areas. In one brief period following Germany's unsuccessful revolution of 1848, intellectuals, political activists, and reformers came to the United States as political refugees. They became known as the "Greens" — restless, radical, revolutionary. After the Civil War, came a "blueing" of the German immigrant tide as the number of peasants declined and intellectuals and more artisans and factory workers arrived.

As they poured in, the Germans overtook the Irish after 1850 as the largest incoming group of immigrants. In fact, between 1850 and 1860 every second immigrant entering the United States was a German. From then until 1890, the Germans led all immigrants in numbers. By 1900 five million Germans had come to America.

German immigrants spread themselves more widely in America than did any other immigrant group. They confined themselves neither to city nor to country. They were on farms *and* in factories. They swelled the population of burgeoning American cities and tilled millions of acres. They made New York in 1880 the third largest German city in the world (after Berlin and Vienna), and they made Milwaukee into a "German Athens," filled with literary and cultural activities. Meanwhile, they were developing one hundred million American acres on over 670,000 farms.

In the course of their immigration, the Germans, unlike other groups, came from all classes, ranging from peasants to university professors. They even provided a frontier oddity — "Latin farmers," intellectuals who turned to farming in the New World. Just before the Civil War, the American writer and landscape architect Frederick Law Olmstead described the "Latin farmer" at work in Texas: "a figure in blue flannel shirt and pendant beard, quoting Tacitus, having in one hand a long pipe, in the other a butcher's knife." Looking into the farmer's bookcase, he found it "half-filled with classics, half with sweet potatoes."

Thanks to their numbers, their variety, and their traditions, German immigrants added a touch of grace to the American scene, notably in the way Christmas was celebrated. Olmstead described what he saw in pre-Civil War America at Christmastime: "mischief and drunken uproariousness." In Missouri, Christmas was celebrated in American households by firing off guns. As late as 1860, the only businesses in some northern cities that closed to honor Christmas were in the German sections. The atmosphere of the cities was more like Halloween than Christmas.

The Germans imported their tradition of religious festivals, of expressing the joy of religious holy days in celebration, song, and food. It was new to America. Instead of Christmas carousing, the Germans introduced Christmas caroling, added Christmas cakes, and, of course, the *Tannenbaum* or Christmas tree. (For Easter, they added the Easter rabbit, the Easter egg, and egg hunts.)

The German spirit applied to Sunday as well, and here they were at odds with the bluenosed, day-of-gloom view of Sunday that prevailed among "respectable folk." The German "continental Sunday" met the American puritanical Sunday head-on wherever Germans clustered. For the Germans, beer, wine, and song were a natural part of Sunday. They drank but did not get drunk. They sang but were not rowdy. Still, they were festive on Sundays and this offended straitlaced native-born Americans.

Eventually, the German way won out in America, but not

40

before inevitable and unavoidable confrontations with the day-of-gloom Sunday Americans. There were demonstrations, even riots, arrests, protests, and open political struggles. Such was the situation that in 1883 a prominent magazine editor reported the Germans had "two things they insist upon as a class" that ran against the prevailing attitude of native Americans: "the right to drink beer and wine in public places at all times, and the right to amuse themselves on Sunday."

The Germans had a word for it — *Gemutlichkeit,* a convivial, good-natured approach toward life. It was a middle way between the heavy-handed puritanical style that frowned upon any pleasure and the high-pitched hell-raising of frontier America. By the 1880s, the editor of *Northwest Magazine* reported: "The German notion that it is a good thing to have a good time has found a lodgment in the American mind."

The spirit of German newcomers was heard in their singing societies and seen in the *Turnverein* movement of gymnastic societies. The latter were rooted in an early nineteenth-century movement in Germany that aimed at the "ideal of an all-around human being, citizen, and member of society." Further back, it was the Roman notion of a healthy mind in a healthy body. Gymnastics were a means to that end and *Turnvereins* spread wherever Germans did. They became a rallying point for German immigrants and then paramilitary forces when Know-Nothings descended on them. (Generations of school children who, often reluctantly, have had to take gym are testimonials to the *Turner* influence in America.) The *Turner* slogan summed up the Germans in America: *Fisch, From, Froh, Frei* — "Bold, Devout, Gay, Free."

German-Americans were devoted to their group, to their traditions, to their family, and to their faith. Half were Catholics and vigorously so. Allowing for freethinkers and skeptics among them, the rest were predominantly Lutherans and just as vigorously devout. The farmer Diederich, a Lutheran, described how from the very start, before there was any church building, Sunday services were held for "twelve fami-

41

lies living here in the woods, spread over a radius of four miles":

> Sundays we hold a church-meeting at our house; it is a joy to us to see that, weather permitting, people come from as far away as two or three miles to take part in our service and once we had a gathering of 37 people. After saying a few psalms together or singing a few verses out of our old Elberfelder song-book, we pray together. Then a sermon is read, after that some more singing and finally, another prayer. May the Lord Jesus give us his blessing for he must help us a little so that we shall be in a position to build a little church.

For German Catholics, Wisconsin provided a barometer of their devotion and of the support they received from the Old Country. In the eighteen years between its founding and the outbreak of the Civil War in 1861, the Diocese of Milwaukee grew from 15,000 to 190,000 Catholics, with Germans the dominant group. The diocese, which originally comprised the entire state of Wisconsin, was helped considerably by the Ludwig-Missionsverein, founded in Munich under the patronage of King Louis I of Bavaria to help German Catholic immigrants.

The vitality of Wisconsin Catholicism in 1861 is reflected in a report sent back to the Ludwig-Missionsverein in Munich. The diocese went from six priests and four unfinished churches in 1844 to 215 "well-finished" churches, 23 under construction, and 117 priests. The report also stressed the Germans' "special zeal for the Christian education of their children" and praised, in particular, the Bavarian School Sisters who were sending teachers to parishes throughout the Union.

In constructing its seminary, the Milwaukee diocese drew on the support of the other cities in what has been called the German triangle of American Catholicism. The helpful "generosity" of German Catholics in Cincinnati and in St. Louis was welcomed. As the missionary report concluded of German-Catholic efforts: "The little mustard seed has grown into a very promising tree."

Whereas pre-1850 German immigrants were prompted to organize rural colonies to protect their traditional ways, the large number who came later built up a strong system of national parishes. In them, they could feel at home with their faith, traditions, customs, mannerisms, and language. A close-knit tribal feeling enveloped the parishes not only within the German triangle of Milwaukee, St. Louis, and Cincinnati, but also in such cities as Buffalo, Cleveland, and Baltimore.

In Baltimore, for instance, the Redemptorist Fathers, who were particularly committed to German Catholics, spearheaded the growth of parish life. As early as 1859, German Catholics in Baltimore had their own weekly newspaper in their native language. In faith as in hopeful hard work, to be half-hearted was not to be German at all. Wherever they clustered, a complex of church, parish school, parish clubs, and German-language newspapers were not far behind, all of them distinctly and thoroughly German.

As the Germans became a major force in the Catholic Church in America, they fought to preserve their mother tongue and their traditions. They were sensitive to threats to their identity and also about Irish predominance in the Catholic hierarchy. (Described in Chapter 2 on the Irish.) Language was both a factor and a touchy point. Unlike the Irish, who arrived speaking English, the Germans stressed preservation of their language. According to the prominent Church historian Monsignor John Tracy Ellis, the language advantage enabled the Irish "to become assimilated with the native population much faster than the Germans, and it probably was accountable for the fact that more Irish priests than German were selected for the episcopacy at a time when native-born American clergy were still few in numbers."

Irish-German tensions in the Catholic Church came to a climax in the 1890s after complaints were lodged in Rome charging neglect of German Catholics and their needs. The controversial Lucerne Memorial was adopted in 1891 at an international meeting of the St. Raphael Society, which was devoted to the care of German Catholic immigrants. With a militant German layman, Peter Paul Cahensly, playing a leading part, it proposed that parochial schools "should always include the mother tongue" as well as English and, explosively, that Irish get Irish bishops, Italians get Italian bishops, and of course, Germans get German bishops. The delicate and threatening idea of proportional representation in the Catholic Church by nationality also was proposed.

The Lucerne Memorial failed to win papal approval in Rome. In the United States the Cahensly movement was tactfully laid to rest by James Cardinal Gibbons of Baltimore. The Catholic hierarchy rejected out-of-hand charges that they had neglected their flock and Cardinal Gibbons spoke for them. He denounced anyone sowing seeds of dissension in the Catholic Church and added: "Let us glory in the title of American citizen. We owe our allegiance to one country, and that country is America."

The Cahensly movement soon died down, so much so that Cardinal Gibbons invited Cahensly to dinner during the latter's 1910 visit to the United States. When Cahensly went back to Germany he reported "a great improvement of conditions among German Catholics and other immigrants." Meanwhile, the vigor of German-American Catholicism and its loyalty to Rome were evident in national parishes, which were distinctly German and devoutly Catholic.

Whereas German Catholics were pitted against other Catholics who were Irish, German Lutherans became embroiled in controversies with fellow Germans. Among Lutherans, conversions to Catholicism were infrequent. Disputes over doctrine, sacraments, and use of the German language led, however, to the formation of various Lutheran synods, notably the conservative Missouri Synod founded in 1847. With the establishment of Concordia Seminary in St. Louis, the Missouri Synod had an influential base for its program of maintaining an uncorrupted Lutheranism, parochial schools, and use of the German language.

44

In the process of getting settled in America, German Catholics and Lutherans looked to church and clergy, as the Buffalo Historical Society was told in 1880 by the editor of the local German paper: "The very history of the German immigration is indissolubly connected with the German clergy, who were their leaders and advisors."

After the Church, the German press came next in influence. It was by far the most extensive among all immigrant groups. In 1910, there were 786 newspapers among an estimated 2,000 German-language publications in the United States. In several states there were more German-language newspapers than those published by all other immigrant groups combined. The *Die Staats Zeitung und Herold* of New York has been publishing since 1834 under the characteristic slogan "an American paper printed in the German language."

That slogan epitomizes the German immigrant experience during the nineteenth century. The Germans were Americans who spoke German, but less and less so as their immigrant numbers declined after 1890. By the twentieth century, various German groups were raising alarms about the loss of ethnic identity. By then, they were able to take for granted their comfortable place in the New World.

On one hand, German-Americans established the largest nationality organization in the country, the National German-American Alliance, which, fifteen years after its founding, in 1899, had reached a membership of two million. On the other hand, German-Americans felt so accepted that their main concern was a battle against Prohibition. When the German-American Alliance built up a kitty of $1.25 million to fight for the "preservation of personal liberty," only $271 went for German schools. Even less was committed to fighting anti-German feeling in America. It seemed so unnecessary. Ever since the Civil War, German-Americans had been esteemed among all immigrant groups. They were considered reputable and easily assimilated. They were praised as law-abiding and strongly patriotic. In 1903, a sociologist in Boston pronounced the Germans the best ethnic type in the city. In 1908, when a group of professionals were asked to rate the traits of immigrant groups, the Germans were rated above the English. In some respects, they were even rated as superior to native-born Americans. And why not? Their hard work was reaping the harvest of solid economic status. They had largely risen out of the working classes, were businessmen, farmers, clerks, and skilled craftsmen. One report showed that a German-American was more likely to own his home than a native-born American.

With the outbreak of World War I, however, the Fatherland cast a dark shadow on German-Americans. Almost overnight, a wave of hostility, rage, and rioting swept over them. Extremists led attacks on everything German: German language in the schools, German music and literature, singing societies, and even Dachshunds. German foods were renamed. Frankfurters became hot dogs, hamburgers Salisbury steak, sauerkraut Liberty Cabbage.

Despite this, German-Americans made a major contribution to the U.S. war effort and provided its two great military heroes, General of the Armies and commander of the American Expeditionary Force, John J. Pershing, and the air hero Captain Eddie Rickenbacker. Fortunately, the anti-German epidemic subsided just as quickly as it had risen. But it did largely end the clearly-delineated German-American community. "German America, the amorphous community which had existed from 1850 to World War I, collapsed and largely disappeared in the fiery furnace of that war," wrote a leading historian of immigration.

After World War I, the German presence remained pervasive, though it was not prominently labeled as such. The Germans, for one thing, had a celebrated turn at bat in the national pastime as Babe Ruth hit homer after headline homer. Baseball, with its demand on both skill and strength in an almost mathematical framework, was the sport in which Germans starred — from Honus Wagner to Lou Gehrig to Ray

Schalk. Elsewhere, there were two German-American presidents, Hoover and Eisenhower, conservatives like Senator Everett Dirksen and liberals like Arthur Schlesinger, Jr., labor leaders like Walter E. Reuther, millionaires like the Rockefellers, journalists like H. L. Mencken, H. V. Kaltenborn, and Walter Lippmann, literary figures like Theodore Dreiser and John Steinbeck. In the early 1970s, half of all elected governors and U.S. congressmen had German origins. For good measure, as a reminder of the German mixture of morality and fun, there is Charles Schulz, the creator of the wise world of children in *Peanuts.*

In the Catholic Church, German-Americans counted cardinals — Elmer Ritter (St. Louis), Albert Meyer and George Mundelein (Chicago) — and college presidents, bishops, and theologians: Father Theodore Hesburgh (president of Notre Dame); Jesuit theologian Gustave Weigel, S.J.; the bishops of Cleveland, Charleston, Austin, Texas, Grand Rapids, Michigan, and New Ulm, Minnesota.

Except for a brief interruption on their way to acceptance and achievement, German immigrants demonstrated that they also succeed who dig and work, who keep their faith and build on their hope.

4 THE SCANDINAVIANS

Salt of the earth

My dear sisters, it was a bitter cup for me to drink, to leave a dear mother and sister and to part forever in this life, though living. Only the thought of the coming world was my consolation; there I shall see you all . . . up to the present I cannot deny that homesickness gnaws at me hard. When I think, however, that there will be a better livelihood for us here than in poor Norway, I reconcile myself to it and thank God, who protected me and mine over the ocean's waves and led us to a fruitful land, where God's blessings are daily before our eyes.

Homesick but determined, Henrietta Jessen wrote from Milwaukee to her sisters in Norway on February 20, 1850, describing how she, her husband, and children were doing in America. It had been a tough winter, with her husband sick and unable to work for two months. Fortunately, four Norwegian families living nearby helped the family with both money and articles for the house. "I believe," she wrote, "I may say that even if I had been in my own native town I would hardly have received the help I have had here."

Mixing her faith in God with hope for a new life in America and the charity of fellow Norwegians, Henrietta Jessen was al-

48

ready counting the blessings in her children, the focus of the immigrant family. Her son Seval would give her "happy days, he is so tender and understanding." George is "a little rascal"; Georgine "is large for her age; everybody asks if they are twins." Soren was already demonstrating the characteristic Scandinavian capacity for backbreaking labor: "He has kept us supplied with wood this winter and works like a little horse."

The Jessen family was in the first substantial wave of Scandinavian immigration. The Norwegians began coming in noticeable numbers in the 1840s, the Swedes after 1852, the Finns after the Civil War, and the Danes in the 1880s. As viewed by a journalist in 1887, these nationalities are "so closely allied and have so many common characteristics that few of their neighbors in the [American] West attempt to distinguish them."

Whether Norwegian, Swedish, Finnish, or Danish, the Scandinavians were immediately well-received. Other immigrant groups, holed up in teeming American cities, were criticized and abused, called names, and even attacked. The Scandinavians, who participated in the winning of the West, were sought after. Western states, such as Wisconsin, Iowa, and Minnesota, even established official commissioners of emigration. Such was Minnesota's success that its Board of Emigration reported "a great deal of envy and ill will from people in other States who were interested in seeing the Scandinavian emigration turned toward Kansas and other States."

The Scandinavians were as hardy a breed of newcomers as ever were processed through Castle Garden and Ellis Island. Their taste for adventure reflected their Viking heritage. Their capacity for hard work had been developed in the harsh terrain and stubborn soil of Scandinavia. Their ability to endure was the harvest of survival in the snow, wind, and cold of their homeland. They were ready for the rough and rugged West of America. And that is where they went, to live by the sentiments expressed by a celebrated nineteenth-century Swedish

49

Lutheran minister Gustaf Unonius: "I do not expect to 'cut gold with jackknives.' I am prepared to earn my daily bread by the sweat of my brow."

Looking back from the vantage point of the 1920s, one student of the immigrant process concluded that it was the "consensus of opinion among competent observers that these northern people have been the most useful of the recent great additions to the American race." Throughout commentaries written by both Scandinavians themselves and outside observers, the same traits emerge time after time: hard-working, industrious, thrifty, honest, religious, interested in education, physically sturdy. Not spectacular, but solid. Not daring, but durable. Not poetic, but practical. Historian Carl Wittke describes them as "hardy men and strong women, deeply religious, determined to succeed, not brilliant or spectacular, but the salt of the earth."

Coming from countries with a high rate of literacy (by 1900, illiteracy had been practically wiped out in Scandinavia), they provided a rich account of their immigrant experience, particularly in letters home. Their strong religious feelings, their optimistic view of America, and their determination punctuate these moving firsthand accounts. When read in their former home towns, each letter added to what became known as Scandinavia's nineteenth-century "American fever" and "emigration frenzy." A selection from those letters shows why.

> Since I love you, Tellef, more than all my other brothers and sisters, I feel very sorry that you have to work your youth away in Norway, where it is so difficult to get ahead. There you can't see any results of your labor, while here you can work ahead to success and get to own a good deal of property, even though you did not have a penny to begin with. I wish that you would sell the farm now for what you can get for it and come here as fast as possible. I and all the others with me believe that you would not regret it.

This is a beautiful and fertile country. Prosperity and contentment are almost everywhere. Practically everything needed can be sown or planted here and grows splendidly, producing a yield of many fold without the use of manure.

If God grants my children life and strength, and if they themselves are willing to work, they will be far more fortunate here than in Norway.

In Sweden, a particularly popular nineteenth-century ditty sang of America where

Ducks and chickens rain right down,
A roasted goose flies in,
And on the table lands one more
With knife and fork stuck in.

Scandinavians boarded ships and sailed, later steamed, for an America which offered what these rugged farmers wanted most of all, land. Economic hardship rather than religious or political oppression pushed them to emigrate. Hard times at home grew worse. A number of disastrous harvests between 1850 and 1880 hit Scandinavian farmers. Their growing season was too short, their taxes too high, their families too large to be supported by the harvests. As to jobs, there were too few at wages that were too low.

So they came, two million Scandinavians between 1820 and the outbreak of World War I. Of every 100 of them, 54 were Swedes, 32 Norwegians, and 14 Danes. While Sweden sent the largest number (1.1 million), by 1910, the U.S. Immigration Commission was reporting that Norway had sent a larger proportion of its population to America than any other country except Ireland.

The striking aspect of Scandinavian immigration was that

it traveled in a straight line geographically. Scandinavians settled in the same latitude in America as they lived in in their homelands, with the Norwegians going toward the most northerly areas. The Scandinavians found climate and scenery that was just like home — plus opportunity. For America, they were a providential import, able to handle the rough and tough life of the frontier.

Their trip across the Atlantic itself was tough enough; the one West could be tougher. The inland trip from New York meant going up the Hudson River by steamboat to Albany where they transferred to Erie Canal boats for Buffalo. Next came passage on the Great Lakes for the West. Immigrants reported that the Canal and Lakes boats were harder to take than the ships that had borne them across the ocean. The quarters were so crowded that parents had to stand so their children could use the cramped space to lie down.

Then there were the dangers of fraud at the hands of guides and interpreters and of sickness from the lack of ventilation in the crowded traveling conditions. And always the poverty. One immigrant who became a leading figure in the Middle West recalled the Scandinavian on a levee in the West, "just landed from a steamer, in his short jacket and other outlandish costume, perhaps seated on a wooden box, with his wife and large group of children around him, and wondering how he shall be able to raise enough means to get himself 10 or 20 miles into the country."

The railroads as well as the individual states wanted the Scandinavians to come West — the railroads because it was good business, the states because it was good for the development of empty stretches of land. The Scandinavians, in fact, offered a double benefit for the railroads. They furnished the labor to lay the tracks and then they settled down to farm the land, providing business in the form of transportation of both people and produce.

As the Scandinavians pushed farther and farther west, they traveled like land-bound Vikings whose ships were covered wagons and whose seas were the seemingly endless American prairies. The land rolled on and on and the caravan of wagons creaked along across its vastness. The high grass parted as the wagons passed, then straightened up again behind them, as would the seas. On and on, the caravans pushed in pursuit of land where the Scandinavians would strike their new roots in America.

When their wagon journeys ended, the Scandinavians built sod huts and, later, log cabins. Cool in summer, warm in winter, the sod house was substantial enough to last for about six years. Built up against a slope, its dirt floor two or three steps beneath the door, it admitted light through the door and permitted smoke to go out through a hole in the dirt roof. Log stumps served as stools and an immigrant's trunk often became a dining table. Beds consisted of straw mattresses on hard boards or springs of taut cords. The hut had one room, which was a little higher than a strapping Scandinavian and about twelve by fourteen feet in size.

In winter, the western snow storms were so staggering that wires had to be strung between the hut and the barn so that the farmers could find their way back and forth. In other seasons, a prairie fire could be "terrifying," as a frontier Norwegian mother of ten, Mrs. Gro Svendsen, wrote home from Iowa in 1863: "It is a strange and terrible sight to see all the fields a sea of fire. Quite often the scorching flames sweep everything along in their path — people, cattle, hay, fences."

In all this, Scandinavian farmers were starting from scratch, dependent on what they brought from across the ocean in the way of tools, meager funds, and the strength of their bodies. Homestead and harvest were hostage to the decisions they made and the work they did. Living as many as fifty miles from the nearest mill and twenty-five miles from the nearest town, each family had to be an island unto itself. The sun scorched, the snow chilled, and the family earned its daily bread literally by the "sweat of its brow."

While Scandinavian men carried a backbreaking burden of

manual work, the women performed prodigies. The wife did the housework, bore and cared for the children, prepared meals, helped with the livestock, churned the butter, made the soap, canned, prepared cheese, wove, dyed, mended, sewed, prayed, and held the family together.

The strong link between family and faith was epitomized by Gro Svendsen when she wrote home of "our sacred duties as parents and the heavy responsibilities laid upon us" and cited the advice of her brother, Ole Nielsen: "We should rear the children to the best of our understanding and ability, and then leave the rest to Him who said, 'For of such is the Kingdom of Heaven.' "

Writing home to Norway from Estherville, Iowa, Nielsen himself summarized the way in which Scandinavian settlers viewed their hard lot within a religious perspective. He expressed thanks "to our Lord and Creator . . . that He lets us experience both good and bad luck, want and tribulation, but also that He in His goodness, if only we have the wisdom to understand it, blesses our labor." He added: "As the poet has said: 'All will prove fruitful to those who truly love God.' "

Scandinavians in America had what one commentator called "land hunger." Even when they had no capital, they worked as laborers, saved their money, and waited for the chance to buy land, a yoke of oxen or a team of horses, and some basic farm implements. With the Homestead Act of 1862, land could be obtained cheaply, particularly in the Northwest.

A Minnesota farmer named Levor Timanson provides a typical example of how Scandinavians satisfied their "land hunger" by waiting, working, and moving West. He emigrated in 1848 with his father, arriving in Wisconsin at the age of eighteen. Then he worked for five years as a farm laborer, carpenter, and mason before visiting Iowa and Minnesota in search of suitable land. He decided to settle in Minnesota as a stock and grain farmer and owned 840 acres by 1882, with 550 of them under cultivation.

A 1901 study found that 64 percent of Norwegians were involved in farming, a pattern that persisted into the second generation with the same proportion. This was more than twice as high as that among second-generation Germans. Second-generation Danes and Swedes also had a penchant for farming, though not as pronounced: 50 percent of the Danes, 43 percent of the Swedes. In all three Scandinavian groups, the percentage increased from the first to the second generation.

Even those Scandinavians who did not farm tended to enter occupations related to the land, its products, or its tools. Many, for example, were lumberjacks. Some writers contended that several feats attributed to the legendary Paul Bunyan were based on stories told by early Swedish lumberjacks. Some of them became operators of lumber mills. Swedes were in demand as mechanics and furniture-makers. Many Norwegians worked in the copper and iron mines near Lake Superior and others in the fisheries, in keeping with their occupation at home. Most halibut fishermen were Norwegians and still others became involved in whale and salmon fishing. Some worked as seamen and ships' captains, particularly on the Great Lakes.

As settlers on the land who needed all the help they could get, Scandinavian farmers put a premium on large families. Children helped with the many chores as they grew up and, once grown, could settle on nearby homesteads. Families of ten and twelve were not unusual and some reached sixteen, eighteen, or even twenty-four.

By appearance, by democratic attitude, by outlook, and by religion, the Scandinavians took root quickly in America. They were attuned to democratic government and were steadfastly Protestant. Just as "Irish" automatically implied Democrat and Catholic, "Scandinavian" indicated Republican and Lutheran. Initially, strong anti-slavery feelings drew Scandinavians to the Republican Party, which increased its appeal by advocating free homesteads. This was particularly the case among Norwegians and Swedes, whose Republican affinities still are strong.

The Scandinavian zeal for religion was matched by zest for religious arguments. It was not with others that they fought about their religious beliefs, but among themselves. Schism, controversy, factionalism, and feuds marked the religious scene, especially among the Norwegians. By 1860, they already had six different synods in America, a total that grew to fourteen as they argued and split up over theological issues and factional disputes. Often, a newly-arrived Norwegian immigrant would have three or four different Lutheran churches to choose from in a single community.

The Norwegians also became embroiled with Swedish Lutherans over such matters as ministerial garb, penance, and altar service and over their different national identities. They attacked the Augustana group of Swedish Lutherans for Americanizing too rapidly, splitting off to form a Norwegian-Danish organization, which in turn split into two independent synods. Within the Danish Lutheran Church, splits and factions were generated by various controversies, particularly the issue of using the Danish language.

By contrast, the Swedes have had basically their one Augustana Synod. Their Lutheranism was particularly stern and straitlaced, even puritanical, largely as a reaction against the laxness that was criticized in the Lutheran Church of Sweden. Dancing, cards, drinking, secret societies, and the theater were condemned as the works of the devil. In general, Lutheranism among the Scandinavian immigrants was stricter than it was in their mother churches.

The Lutheran enthusiasm of Scandinavians spawned both schools and newspapers whose numbers were increased by the factional disputes. According to one commentator: "A separate denominational school and a family paper seem to be indispensable parts of the machinery of every newly organized sect, no matter how young or how small or how poor it may be."

By 1893, there were 36 Scandinavian colleges, schools, and seminaries. Minnesota alone had 16 and added four more by

1900. The Norwegians had 19 colleges by 1920. The Scandinavian press also proliferated, with Swedish-language publications alone reaching 1,200 at one point. That total dropped in the early decades of this century, but there were still 300 Swedish publications prior to World War I. Between 1850 and 1925, the Norwegians established over 400 newspapers as well as other types of publications. They have had newspapers in their native tongue continuously since 1847, including *Nordisk Tidende*, which is still being published in the "Little Norway" of Brooklyn's Bay Ridge section. Among the newspapers established by the Finns, *The Amerikan Sanomet* of Ashtabula, Ohio, dates back to 1884.

Viewed within the context of the American "melting pot," the Scandinavians have been a silent ethnic group. Even their most famous sons and daughters did not carry a well-known ethnic label. There has been, for example, little ethnic fanfare about two of the most famous Swedish-Americans: Charles A. Lindbergh, hero of the first nonstop transatlantic flight, and Carl Sandburg, celebrated poet and biographer of Abraham Lincoln. Or about Jacob Riis, the Danish immigrant of 1870 who became a famous journalist and urban reformer.

Except for Florida, California, and Washington, D.C., Scandinavian-Americans stayed primarily in the northern parts of the United States where they originally settled. Their ethnic capitals have become Chicago and Minneapolis-St. Paul. In terms of individual nationalities, Chicago has the largest concentration of Swedes and Minneapolis and New York of Norwegians. The largest number of Danes are in the Los Angeles area and Chicago and of Finns in Michigan.

From time to time, commentators have taken particular notice of Scandinavian athletic prowess, as when the well-known sportswriter Grantland Rice wrote: "The teams out West, especially the Minnesota teams, are the most feared of our American teams, solely for the Norse power supplied to them by the huge muscular Swedes with which they are amply staffed."

The Norwegians brought skiing to America, but not for sport. It was an efficient way to get around in the ice and snow of the West. It was recorded as early as 1841 in Rock Prairie, Wisconsin. In the 1850s, John "Snowshoe" Thompson made a deal to carry the U.S. mail on homemade skis across a virtually impassable stretch of ninety wintry miles between Placerville, California, and Carson Valley, Idaho. For twenty years, he was a celebrated mail-carrying skier. By the 1880s, function had turned to fun as the sport of skiing started to spread. The National Ski Association was formed in 1904.

As early as 1855, Swedish gymnastics, which is based on principles of massage and physiotherapy developed early in the century, was introduced in New York. Gymnastic groups were formed in America and for a time the Swedish system of gymnastics was in use at the U.S. Naval Academy in Annapolis. Swedish massage and physiotherapy are still much in demand.

The Scandinavians, like other immigrant groups, formed societies built on nationality. The Norwegians, for example, organized *Bygdelags*, social groups of immigrants from the same districts in Norway. The Sons of Norway, founded in Minneapolis in 1895, had a wider reach, but a similar aim of staying in touch with national origins, culture, and history. Both the Norwegians and the Swedes are fond of singing and have formed singing societies. Their colleges also strike a musical note in their academic programs and in their choirs, as at St. Olaf's in Minnesota, Bethany in Kansas, and Augustana in Illinois.

After its founding in 1887, the Danish Folk Society flourished in its aim to unite all the Danes in America "who desire to maintain the Danish character." It stressed the twofold benefits of its work — to the Old Country and to the new — as have all Scandinavian and other nationality societies.

As the Scandinavians Americanized, they both retained and reflected their individual national traits. Although they get along with each other, Scandinavians do take seriously the differences among themselves. Separate newspapers, churches, societies, and schools, for example, have reflected the fact that Swedes, Norwegians, Danes, and Finns represent different languages, traditions, and Old Country experiences. They cannot be automatically lumped together in prayer or song. (The United Scandinavian Singers of America, organized in 1886, split over Swedish, Norwegian, and Danish differences after giving only three festivals.)

There is both a push and a pull, both a tendency to come together as Scandinavians and an awareness of the differences among them in America as at home. In his landmark study of Scandinavian-Americans, published in 1914, Professor Kendric Babcock characterized the differences this way: "The typical Swede is aristocratic, fond of dignities, assertive: he is polite, vivacious, and bound to have a jolly time without troubling too much about the far future. . . ."

"The Norwegian," he wrote, "is above all democratic. He is simple, serious, intense, severe even to bluntness, often radical and visionary, and with a tendency to disputatiousness. . . . The Dane is the Southerner of the Scandinavians, but still a conservative. He is gay, but not to excess. . . . He is preeminently a small farmer or trader, honest and persevering, ready and easy-going, and altho not given to great risks, he is quick to see a bargain and shrewd in making it."

Yet, as became clear after the large waves of immigration ceased, all of them remained not so much stubbornly Swedish, Norwegian, Danish, Finnish, or even simply Scandinavian, they became predominantly American.

5 THE ITALIANS

Heroes all around me;
I never saw them

The feste and the processions in the old country, in Lombardy, oh, I used to love them. In Bugiarno everybody was reverent to the Madonna and the saints. . . . Everybody had a grand time. But when they carried the Madonna out from the church, all was quiet — everybody was reverent. But the feste the Italian people make here in Chicago, me, I think with Father Alberto, it's not right. It's not right to take the Holy Madonna out in the streets of Chicago where so many people have not our religion. The American men smoke and chew and keep on the hat when the Holy Virgin goes by. That's not right!

In *Rosa: The Life of An Italian Immigrant,* an Italian woman from a town near Milan was reacting to the cold and alien soil in which she and her fellow immigrants were planting their sun-drenched Catholicism. They brought over an exuberant, emotional, demonstrative faith which burst forth in festivals dedicated to patron saints. Like flowers struggling to bloom, the festivals personified the Catholicism of those who came from Italy as the last large wave of immigrants.

Without their festivals, "religion was cold, formal, and lacking significance," sociologist Joseph Lopreato has pointed out. With their festivals, Italian immigrants faced disapproval from native-born Americans and from Irish-Catholics, who had preceded them in the waves of immigration. Two religious styles rubbed against each other: the legalistic and puritanical one of the Irish and the easygoing and affectionate one of the Italians.

An Irish pastor on New York's Lower East Side expressed typical disapproval when he wrote to the archbishop in the summer of 1892 about a festival in honor of St. Donatus. His description included the ingredients of an Italian religious festival: church services followed by a procession in the streets which culminated in music, singing, feasting, and fireworks. In honoring St. Donatus, the procession was held "with all the noise of brass bands and fireworks in the streets of the 6th and 14th wards." A priest from Piacenza, Italy, accompanied by four altar boys, paraded behind the brass band. "Then came the statue of St. Donatus carried on the shoulders of four men. Women and small girls followed with large and small candles and the men of the society brought up the rear."

The Irish had trouble accepting this religious style of the many Italian immigrants who started arriving after 1880. The Italians followed them into the cities and, suddenly, the Irish faced a different brand of their universal faith. All the cities with large Irish populations were receiving a large number of Italians, particularly New York, Boston, Philadelphia, Chicago, Baltimore, and Detroit. By 1920, eighty-five percent of Italian immigrants lived in the eight states where seventy-five percent of the Irish had settled.

Fifty years separated the peak decades of Irish and Italian immigration. Whereas more than 900,000 Irish arrived in the decade between 1851 and 1860, more than 2 million Italians arrived in the first ten years of this century. Only 80,000 Italians arrived before 1880, but almost another 5 million had joined them by 1930, four-fifths of them from southern Italy.

"The land literally hemorrhaged peasants," writes Erik Amfitheatrof, a chronicler of the massive migration. Out of a population of 14 million in southern Italy when the country was unified between 1860 and 1870, over one-third (5 million) emigrated by the beginning of World War I. At one point as many as 5,000 immigrants a day, seven days a week, were going through Ellis Island. "The exodus of southern Italians from their villages at the turn of the twentieth century has no parallel in history," he notes.

The Italians migrated to break the chains of poverty. They had worked from sunrise to sunset to eke out an existence for their large families. The soil had been harsh and unresponsive, their farming methods primitive, the feudal system crushing. The *contadino*, or peasants, were ground under by the village elite and if they went forth to get jobs the pay was only a few cents for twelve or more hours.

Meanwhile, America beckoned. Arriving in 1907, one immigrant found that "New York was like a dream. We couldn't believe our eyes." He saw a huge chunk of beef on display: "I had never eaten a piece of beef before. . . . I used to work from sunrise to sunset to eat wild herbs and beans . . . I'll never forget how I longed for that chunk of beef."

Poor and hopeful when they left, Italian immigrants were poor and bewildered when they arrived. They were faced with what one historian has described as "a debilitating sense of always having to measure themselves by Anglo-Saxon values and standards." Uneducated and unskilled, they came with almost-empty pockets. (In 1910, the average Italian immigrant arrived with only seventeen dollars.) Their American survival and adjustment centered on their religious faith and, particularly, on their family life.

The religious festivals symbolized both that faith and their ties to the Old Country. At home, each town had its own patron saint. Although all else might have been left behind, the Italian immigrants brought along devotion to that patron saint. So unlike the Irish with their *one* saint, Patrick, the Italians had a litany of saints and matching festivals, such as two of the major ones in New York City. In July there is the Feast of the Madonna del Carmine and in September the Feast of San Gandolfo, patron of the little Sicilian town of Polizzi Generosa.

In 1890, the journalist and social reformer Jacob Riis marveled at the number of feast days celebrated by New York Italians. "By what magic the calendar of Italian saints was arranged so as to bring so many birthdays within the season of American sunshine I do not know," he wrote. "But it is well. The religious fervor of our Italians is not to be pent up within brick walls . . . sunshine and flowers belong naturally to it. . . . To the Italian who came over the sea the saint remains the rallying-point in his civic and domestic life to the end of his days . . . the saint means home and kindred, neighborly friendship in a strange land . . . in the numbered streets of Little Italy uptown, almost every block has its own village of mountain or lowland, and with the village its patron saint, in whose worship or celebration — call it what you will — the particular camp makes reply to the question, 'Who is my neighbor?' "

Among Italian immigrants, nothing was more important than the family. It was the seat of emotions, loyalties, and responsibilities. The typical model was the southern Italian peasant family where the father represented power and the mother love. The intense Italian devotion to the Madonna was reflected in strong devotion to the mother. For the father as head, respect was all-important. For the individual, it meant placing the self second, the family first.

Inevitably, in confronting the bewildering adjustment to America, the Italian family faced pressures that undermined parental authority and confounded the older generation. Children of immigrants were torn between two worlds and had trouble seeing that the immigrants in the cities were pioneers just as much as those who had gone West and settled the frontier.

In a sensitive novel on immigrant life, *The Fortunate Pilgrim,* Mario Puzo writes: "They were pioneers, though

63

they never walked an American plain and never felt real soil beneath their feet. They moved in a sadder wilderness, where the language was strange, where their children became members of a different race. It was a price that must be paid."

That price was evident in the way the second generation began to regard immigrants from Italy. They felt embarrassed and awkward as they rushed to look, act, and seem American — which invariably meant Anglo-Saxon. In an evocative essay on the immigrant experience, Puzo describes how he grew to admire the immigrants whom he had "hated, then pitied so patronizingly." Yet, they *were* heroes: "Heroes all around me. I never saw them."

Why had he and so many others failed to see them as heroes?

"How could I?" he asks. "They wore lumpy work clothes and handlebar moustaches, they blew their noses on their fingers and they were so short that their high-school children towered over them. They spoke a laughable broken English and the furthest limit of their horizon was their daily bread. Brave men, brave women, they fought to live their lives without dreams. Bent on survival they narrowed their minds to the thinnest line of existence.

"It is no wonder that in my youth I found them contemptible. And yet they had left Italy and sailed the ocean to come to a new land and leave their sweated bones in America. Illiterate Colombos, they dared to seek the promised land. And so they, too, dreamed a dream."

Ironically, the Irish, whom native Americans had once found so strange, were reacting the same way themselves to Italian immigrants. A clash of culture rather than of religious commitment, it led to attitudes such as one expressed in 1917 by an Irish pastor in New York: "The Italians are not a sensitive people like our own." On the Italian side, the Irish parish seemed money-minded. (The Irish, on the other hand, viewed it as pride in supporting the Church.) An Italian priest who had worked for forty years in Italian colonies in six different cities summed up the reaction of Italians toward an Irish church: "One has to pay as in a theater."

Feeling left out in Irish-dominated parishes, sometimes even forced to attend Mass in the church basement, Italians set about establishing their own national parishes. By 1918, they had 580 churches in New York City alone and also had their own churches in rural areas. One 1908 report that covered a vast stretch from Pennsylvania to South Carolina found 300,000 Italians spread out, yet served by 40 churches. It described the folk quality of the Italian faith and the way in which family life and church celebration were blended together, finding "religious processions, the so-called 'parades' of the Societies. . . . Above all, [are] the banquets; they are tendered on all occasions, opportune and inopportune, for marriages, baptisms, to celebrate the feasts of patron saints, for the departure of a barber who goes to spend a couple of months in Italy and then to celebrate his return. . . . For funerals one spends fabulous sums: one has even seen processions of forty carriages for the funeral of a new-born baby."

In the cities, ethnic parishes were embedded in Little Italies, Little Sicilies, Little Calabrias. As earlier immigrant groups moved uptown to better quarters, the Italians moved in as the latest newcomers at the bottom of the ladder. In Italian parish and ghetto, familiarity bred reassurance, but also offered halfway houses to Americanization.

In such urban ghettos, the dream of the New World was darkened by a life of dirt, destitution, and even danger. New York's first Little Italy, Mulberry Bend, was described in an official report as a place where "new arrivals lived in damp basements, leaky garrets, clammy cellars and outhouses and stables converted into dwellings. Every foot of the 'Bend' reeked with abject misery, cruelty, shame, degradation, and crime. By day a purgatory of unrelieved squalor, at night the 'Bend' became an inferno tenanted by the very dregs of humanity."

At one point, Italian immigrants in New York City lived at

a density of 1,100 to the acre. There were sections in which 1,230 people crowded into 120 rooms, an average of more than 10 persons to a room. At best, there was only space to sleep and eat. In a report on one block where 3,500 people lived, not one bathtub was found, only one family had a hot water range, all the halls were cold and dirty and most of them dark as well. One child in nine died before reaching the age of five.

In the crowded Italian ghetto, it was noted, life in the streets was lived under the "pressure of baby cart on push-cart." It was a staggering sight for an outsider, such as the industrial arts teacher who wrote in 1921 of her first day teaching at a Newark, New Jersey, school in a typical "Little Italy": "My eyes sought everything in bewilderment and curiosity." All the shop signs in Italian . . . bakeries with long or round loaves of Italian bread displayed . . . small boys on the way home clutching the loaves . . . swarthy young men hanging out on street corners . . . men playing cards in the saloons . . . florists and undertaking parlors displaying set pieces of artificial flowers . . . pushcarts moving through crowded sidewalks . . . the unbridled pandemonium of street life.

A 1904 description of Philadelphia's "Little Italy" tells of about thirty-five blocks where the "Italians are closely packed together. One can walk the streets for considerable distances without hearing a word of English. The black-eyed children rolling and tumbling together, the gaily colored dresses of the women and the crowds of street vendors all give the neighborhood a wholly foreign appearance."

Just as the Irish had once been criticized for sticking together as a reaction against being rejected so were the Italians. Writing on "How It Feels to Be a Problem," an eloquent spokesman for the immigrants, Gino C. Speranza, issued a challenge that America was not ready to meet in 1904: to reach out and accept the immigrants. "It is with this in mind that I say that if my countrymen here keep apart, if they herd in great and menacing city colonies, if they do not learn your language, if they know little about your country, the fault is as much yours as theirs. And if you wish to reach us you will have to batter down some of the walls you have yourselves built to keep us from you."

Inside their city colonies, their Little Italies, the Italians were fragmented by narrow loyalties, divided by the gap between northern and southern Italians, and victimized by the infamous *padrone* system. It centered on the campaign to recruit Italians to fill America's booming manpower needs. That recruiting was done by a profiteering Italian who "knew the ropes."

The *padrone*, or labor recruiter, acted as a middleman for employers or eventually operated on his own. He lined up workers in Italy, getting money for passage to America, collecting a fee for finding a job, and making arrangements all along the line. He could inflate charges as well as exact fees, leaving the Italian immigrant up to his strong neck in debt. At about the turn of the century it was estimated that two out of three Italian immigrants in New York were tied into the *padrone* system.

The Italians thus took over from the Irish the backbreaking work of an expanding America. They were the construction laborers, laboring with their hands as they earlier had worked for the stubborn harvest back home. By 1900, almost all those building the New York subway system were Italian. The ranks of street cleaners and garbage collectors, railroad laborers and ditch diggers were filled by Italian immigrants, as were the least desirable jobs in steel plants and glass and shoe factories. There was also a floating population of Italians who provided temporary and seasonal manpower throughout the country.

In the Little Italies of America, familiar figures began to appear: the pushcart vendor of fruits and vegetables, the shoemaker, the iceman, and the barber. The man at the pushcart evolved into the grocery owner and eventually into the wholesale food distributor. The Italian barber shop was analogous to the Irish saloon (though Italian immigrants were by no means teetotalers). Sunday morning was the favorite time to visit the barber shop to exchange news about the Old Country and to take pride in Enrico Caruso and Rudolph Valentino. As everyone's friend, the barber reigned in his neighborhood gathering place, mixing his natural Italian sociability with his pride in his haircutting skills.

Again, like the Irish, the Italians shied away from farming. They lacked both money and will to go West. It was, after all, the brutal life of an Italian peasant farmer that they had left behind. On the farm in the Old Country, they had been humiliated and brutalized. They did not come across the ocean to be farmers but to get jobs in American cities. That was what labor recruiters were urging in Italy and their message stuck.

Immigrants from northern and southern Italy regarded each other suspiciously, with northerners looking down on southerners. Americans picked up on this, particularly since southern Italians arrived poorer, less schooled, and less skilled than the northerners. The latter were regarded as energetic, ambitious, and enterprising; the former as genial, easygoing, more in love with life than with money. The U.S. Immigration Commissioner even went so far as to maintain separate figures for northern and southern Italians, a breakdown that was made for no other group. In keeping with the Anglo-Saxon bias of America, Henry Cabot Lodge praised the northern Italian as having "Teutonic" blood and belonging "to a people of Western civilization."

The fragmentation of Italian immigrants went much further. Coming from a country which had not been united until late in the nineteenth century, they had a sense of village loyalty rather than of national patriotism. It was called *campanilismo*, merging the words for bell and church tower and meaning that their world extended only as far as the church bell could be heard. This attitude came over on the boat. Once here, it was natural for Italians to settle among others from the same village. They often even went to the same block and tenement.

In Buffalo, New York, for instance, Italian immigrants from Abruzzi e Molise in south-central Italy settled on East Delavan Avenue; those from Calabria in southern Italy on Hopkins Street; those from Campania, whose capital is Naples, on North and South Division Streets. In New York, Neapolitans and Calabrians clustered in Mulberry Bend; Genoese along Baxter Street; Sicilians on Elizabeth Street; Piedmontese and Lombards west of Broadway.

Italians banded together into mutual benefit societies which were as abundant as their splintered groupings. By 1910, New York City alone had more than two thousand of them. The spirit of *campanilismo* kept Italian-Americans from joining ranks to achieve the strength of their numbers. In particular, it held them back in developing political muscle.

Many Italians had a particular reason for sticking close to fellow villagers and for being slow to learn English and become naturalized citizens. They were planning to work hard, save their money, and return to Italy to buy land or start a business. They were the "birds of passage" of the immigration tides. As many as 1.2 million Italian immigrants returned to Italy between 1908 and 1916.

Though most Italian immigrants stayed (including many who had intended to return), they did not rush to sink roots. They concentrated on getting jobs and earning money. Their dreams had blurred images that mixed Italy and the United States; their nightmare was the way America changed their children.

An immigrant from Reggia, Calabria, has described his dismay when his son was detoured from working and forced to go to school. That was not the family's plan. The father and his twelve-year-old son had come to New York in 1907 to carry on the father's trade of tool grinding and to save enough to return home and open a small business. They had scraped together forty dollars and left for America, arriving with four dollars and the father's instruments. They immediately set to work after settling in Coney Island with other Calabrians.

69

Each day, except Sunday, they set out at 9:00 A.M. and made their rounds until sunset. On Sunday, little Joe would shine shoes. His father planned to set him up in a second route as a tool grinder. Then it happened: he faced what he called "the American law which compels all smart and all dopey ones to go to school, regardless of whether they want to or need it."

To peasants who had come from a land without hope and without schooling for their children, it seemed insane for an able-bodied son to go to school instead of earning his own way. "Mind you," said the father, "a fellow who was thinking of girls and was strong as a good sized tree could go to school as if he were a nobleman's son, while his poor father was breaking his back."

Eventually, the Calabrian father stayed in America and brought over his wife and two other children. But he never forgot that first crisis. Joe stayed in school until he was fourteen, then quit, "but he was not the same Joe anymore." His father expressed the reactions of other immigrants as the public school struck hard at Old Country ways through the children it was "Americanizing": "The school rather harmed him and ruined my entire life. All the respect and obedience he had before, he lost in the school which did not teach him anything good."

The public school became an enemy of the traditional family-centered life of Italian immigrants. As another immigrant said in expressing a typical reaction: "The schools made of our children persons of leisure — *signorini* ["little gentlemen"] — they lost the dignity of good children to think first of their parents, to help them whether they need it or don't need it. . . . America took from us our children."

The dilemma was very real for the Italian immigrant: school was mandatory and it was also a threat to the core of Italian immigrant life, the family. The American school as an Americanizer meant the upholding of Anglo-Saxon attitudes and preferences, the looking down on immigrant ways. It made rebels of the children of immigrants, rebels against family authority and culture and seekers after worlds outside the family. It also took away the earning power of the young and forced the family to support them. An added irony was that the schools ended up encouraging immigrant children to take up trades — which could be learned faster and better as working apprentices rather than as pupils in classrooms.

Leonard Covello, who became one of New York City's leading educators, recalled how the *i* was dropped from his name by a schoolteacher early in this century and how little he had understood the fact's significance. But his parents did. The son felt his name was "more American" that way. The father knew what it meant — that "you don't change a family name." The mother said: "A person's life and his honor is in his name. He never changes it. A name is not a shirt or a piece of underwear." It was one of the few times the son had dared to oppose his father. Later the same evening, he was standing dejectedly under the gas light on the corner.

"But they don't understand!" he exclaimed to his sister.

"Maybe some day, you will realize that *you* are the one who does not understand," she answered.

Out of such remembrances the second and third generations moved toward an American style that was both loss and gain. The longer they remained the more "American" they became and the more they resembled other American Catholics, especially Irish-Americans. Then, gradually, they rebuilt the ethnic pride that had been undermined by the harsh reception it received in America.

They could thank America for freeing them from the economic and social tyranny of Italy, as summed up by Rosa, the immigrant from Lombardy, quoted earlier. She dreamed of going back to Italy just once before she died, back to the village where she had been put down as inferior. "Now," she said, "I speak English good like an American. I could go anywhere — where millionaires go and high people." She longed to confront the high and mighty of her village who had rejected her. "I wouldn't be afraid. They wouldn't dare hurt me now I

71

come from America. Me, that's why I love America. That's what I learned in America: not to be afraid."

Eventually, Italian-Americans would overcome what two students of their experience have described as nativist prejudice that "bore down especially hard and frequently with a viciousness that seems bizarre today." After the massacre of eleven Italians in New Orleans by a mob bent on avenging the murder of the police chief, Italians were periodic victims of mob violence. There were mob fatalities in 1893, 1895, 1896, 1899, 1901, 1906, 1910, 1914, and 1915 from Denver to Tampa, Florida, and from Marion, North Carolina, to Johnson City, Illinois.

Individuality and ambition prevailed among the Italians, but focused on the family as a unit achieving success, not on one enterprising loner going off to strike it rich. Single-minded and self-centered success in the Protestant, Anglo-Saxon style did not flower among Italians. The individual looked to the family and its approval and the family did not approve success in isolation. Nathan Glazer and Daniel Patrick Moynihan touched the core of this attitude toward success when they commented: "Perhaps the ideal is the entertainer — to give him a name, Frank Sinatra — who is an international celebrity, but still the big-hearted, generous, unchanged boy from the block."

An immigrant from Naples, Stefan Miele, who came early in the twentieth century and found the chance to become a lawyer that he never could have had in Italy, wrote perceptively in 1920 of the gap between Anglo-Saxon and Italian. With an openness that non-Italians usually did not have, he could see both sides. Noting that America is "a wonderful nation," he added that it was a mistake to "assume that the Anglo-Saxon is the perfect human being." There are faults and splendid qualities on both sides — something that only belatedly was acknowledged when ethnic identity came to be respected.

Whereas the Anglo-Saxon is "pre-eminently a business man, an executive, an organizer, energetic, dogged," the Italian finds in him "a lack of the things that go to make life worth living." Even Italians who returned home independent and prosperous had lost something — "a certain light-heartedness, a joy in the little things — the old jest no longer made them laugh." What the Italian had was "the artistic, the emotional temperament, a gift for making little things put sunshine into life, a gift for the social graces."

Italian immigrants brought that grace and that sunshine into American cities and American Catholic churches. On the streets there were religious festivals, on stage, music, particularly grand opera. After a number of attempts to introduce opera on a permanent basis, starting in 1833, Italian opera flowered with the opening of the Metropolitan Opera House in New York in 1883, especially in the years when it was under the management of Guilio Gatti-Casazza. In opera there was no one like the tenor Enrico Caruso and in the movies no one like Rudolph Valentino. Behind such famous Italians there were more than five million immigrants and, eventually, some twenty million Italian-Americans.

For other immigrant groups, the parable of their American adjustment might best be told in terms of power, success, and recognition. For the Italians, it is more suitable to single out one immigrant, such as Salvatore Tarascio, who came to America as a grown man when Teddy Roosevelt was in the White House and who watched on television as man walked on the moon. In him, his children, grandchildren, and great-grandchildren, the theme of Italian immigration is reflected in a pattern of hard work and deep emotions of family and faith.

When he was 101 in 1972, Salvatore Tarascio showed a visitor the workshop in the basement of his Winsted, Connecticut, home. He was still working there: "I've always been capable of doing anything with my hands I could see with my eyes. . . . When you work, the blood comes good."

When he sits in his living room, he is surrounded by photos of weddings, parties, and other family gatherings. His daugh-

73

ter, Carmella, took early retirement "so I could be with Poppa."

When evening comes, Salvatore prays at a shrine he built in his backyard and dedicated to his late wife, Gaetana. "He has a deep devotion to Our Lady," says Carmella. "He goes to Mass every Sunday; there's no holding him back."

"Happy," says the Italian immigrant who in 1903 came for good to America at the age of thirty-three. "Always happy. Never gotta trouble for anybody. I was good for everybody. Everybody likes me. I like everybody. I always do everything I wanted. I enjoy all of it, all of it."

6 THE POLES

A great people for work

I am well enough. I receive now $16 for this month. I don't feel lonesome, because there are two of us girls in this household. The master and mistress are Polish. We are near a church and they send us every Sunday at 6 o'clock in the morning to the mass. We have every day 18 rooms to clean, and to cook and to wash linen. It is myself who washes every week about 300 pieces of linen, and iron it. . . . I iron 4 days, from 6 A.M. to 8 P.M. I do nothing but iron those 4 days. Dear parents, you admonish me so severely to be on my guard. But I cannot and do not walk about the city.

On November 20, 1911, the same day that a letter from her parents arrived, Aleksandra Rembiénska answered with a description of her job as a maid in a Brooklyn, New York, home. She worked hard from 6:00 A.M. until 8:00 P.M., stayed close to home, saved her money, and made plans to bring over her brothers and sisters from Poland. Whenever possible she went to visit Uncle and Aunt Kubacz and, of course, went to Mass every Sunday.

In a stream of letters, Polish immigrants beckoned members of their family and friends to follow them to America: "If a man will work, he need never go hungry." "Here it is not asked what or who was your father, but the question is, what are you?" "And now I will write you how I am getting along. am getting along very well. I have worked in a factory and I am now working in a hotel. I receive (in our money 32) dollars a month and that is very good. If you would like it we could bring Wladzio over some day. We eat here every day what we get only for Easter in our country."

A major part of the "new" immigration of the late nineteenth and early twentieth century, the Poles constituted the largest number of Slavic immigrants. They began arriving in significant numbers after the American Civil War. There were only 50,000 Poles and ten Polish parishes in America in 1870. Five years later, they totaled 200,000, spread over 300 communities and supporting 50 parishes. By 1889, 800,000 were supporting 132 churches and 122 schools, concentrated in six states: New York, Pennsylvania, Massachusetts, Illinois, Michigan, and Wisconsin. By 1920, there were at least three million of Polish parentage in the United States, a number hard to pin down since they were not always listed as Poles upon arrival.

What happened in Buffalo, New York, was typical. Polish immigrants rushed to build a church where they expressed their national identity as well as their faith. As an early historian of the Polish-American experience pointed out in 1922, "A good Pole is expected to be a good Catholic."

In Buffalo, on the same day that John Pitass was ordained at Niagara University, St. Stanislaus Parish was organized. And on the bitterly cold Buffalo day of January 25, 1874, its 300-seat frame church opened, the forerunner of a towering twin-spired structure that today is the spiritual center of America's second largest Polish community. By 1900, St. Stanislaus had 30,000 parishioners and St. Stanislaus Kostka in Chicago more than 50,000. Each parish was thus larger in size than many dioceses.

Dr. Francis F. Fronczak, Buffalo health commissioner from 1910 to 1946, recalled going to St. Stanislaus Church as a boy. He remembered "the crooked muddy stream by the church, the marshes in the neighborhood, and the nearest building some distance away." He also remembered the two school classes set up in the rear of the church. "I remember them well, for it was there I received the foundation of what knowledge I may have today."

Wherever they settled, the Poles made their church the center of *Polonia* (Polish-America). There, devotion to God and to Poland was celebrated in liturgy and language, in the support of their clergy, in use and teaching of the Polish language, and in devoted pursuit of their identity.

Poles introduced American Catholicism to their Paschal Communion cards, the blessing of food on Holy Saturday, and the breaking of the wafers (*oplatki*) at the Christmas Evening meal. The uniquely Polish and poignant "Bitter Lamentations" (*Gorzkie Zale*) was sung at Lenten devotions and the "small hours" of Our Lady's Office were chanted before Sunday High Mass. American Catholicism was enhanced by Polish devotion to the Mother of Christ and, as an observer noted, "Religion permeates the Polish peasant's thought, speech, and daily life. The names of Christ and the Virgin are on his lips all the time."

The parish church became the center for transplanted traditions which were tied both to seasons of the year and to holy days, including:

Christmas Eve, which involved breaking and sharing Christmas wafers among relatives, putting hay underneath the tablecloth or platter, and serving twelve varieties of food.

Holy Week and Easter included beating pots and pans, exhibiting Christ's tomb on Good Friday, bringing Easter foods to church on Saturday for blessing, and dragging Judas through the streets.

Assumption of Mary. Herbs and flowers were brought to church for blessing on "Lady Day."

Zaduzki (All Souls' Day). Food was given to beggars who are supposed to be in touch with the spirits of the dead.

As sociologist Arthur Evans Wood commented in cataloging these and other customs, the Church endowed Polish "work and leisure with a sense of sacredness." Polish immigrants were immersed in their religion. Both men and women exhibited religious fervor. Devotion to their faith was evident in highly-ornamented churches which were centers of imagery, pageantry, and symbolism.

The Polish school was linked to the church as part of the same effort of continuity and survival. In America, the older generations were haunted by the fear that they would "lose" their children in the New World. An observer noted in 1920 that Polish immigrants had "a vague uneasiness that a delicate network of precious traditions is being ruthlessly torn asunder, that a whole world of ideals is crashing into ruins." Polish fathers and mothers had a nightmare: They "picture themselves wandering about lonely in vain search of their lost children."

Kasimir Kozakiewicz, at one time president of the Polish Roman Catholic Union, remembered his grammar school days when "our almost entire school day was conducted in the Polish language" and "only some of the time was devoted to English reading, writing, spelling, history, and geography." He added: "If my memory serves me right we even studied arithmetic in both Polish and English."

What was emerging was a theme summed up by a historian of the Polish-American experience: "Be American but do not lose the Polish touch. Be two men of two cultures rather than one man." In the beginning, Polish immigrants, like other newcomers, huddled together in the strange, cold, crowded environment of American cities. They felt homesick, alienated, and insecure; among their own kind, they felt less of each.

In Buffalo, a young Yale graduate, A. C. Goodyear, headed a 1910 task force investigating the life of 80,000 Poles in that community. His observations were like those made about other immigrant groups: The newcomers were "in the Buffalo

78

community, but they are not of it." The Poles "have their own churches, their own stores and business places, their own newspapers. They are content to live alone and be let alone, and the rest of the population generally knows little about them and cares less."

In the main, uprooted peasants, unskilled (only one in sixteen had a trade) and generally unschooled, Polish immigrants nonetheless were able to offer what post-Civil War America desperately needed — manpower. They were stolid, steadfast, and, in particular, hard-working. Even the most unsympathetic observers, such as a wizened carpenter who spoke to an investigator for Baltimore's Charity Organization Society early in the century, readily conceded that. He had to admit, amidst various uncomplimentary comments, that the Poles are "a great people for work; they work, work, work and then don't know anything to do with the money but hoard it up."

What he failed to note were the main uses for the money saved by Polish immigrants. They used it to bring over other members of the family or to send home and they "developed a perfect mania to acquire a little house and a plot of land" (as historian Carl Wittke has written).

A turn-of-the-century close-up of Baltimore's Polish section along the waterfront offers a composite picture of their traits of hard work, cleanliness, and religious devotion. As viewed by a charity investigator, the life of the Polish immigrant centered on making ends meet. They literally rushed in crowds to the packinghouses when the first fruit and vegetables arrived in the spring. Entire family groups worked there. They peeled (starting at four or five in the morning and staying as late as six in the evening) and they packed (from seven until ten or eleven at night during the rush season). The managers of the packinghouses called the Poles the best workers they ever had. "Even if the whistle is blown at two in the morning, they will come and work with no fooling until five or six at night."

In the summer, families loaded into wagons and headed for canning houses in the country, the women wearing freshly-washed calico dresses, large aprons, and stiff sunbonnets. In the fall and winter, jobs as oyster shuckers beckoned them. With the money earned, they paid landlord, baker, and grocer and, often, at the sacrifice of getting enough food, installment payments were made on homes.

Living in houses described as "cleaner than those occupied by any other group of foreigners," Baltimore's Poles whitewashed the walls once or twice a year, scrubbed the floors, and replaced the stuffing in their mattresses. In their impeccably neat homes, the furniture was at a minimum: a few chairs or boxes, a table, a stove, a bed or two. Children often slept on the floor. Often the only decorations were some colorful dishes on a shelf and "a few cheap prints of religious subjects in elaborate gilt frames on the walls."

Redbirds sang plaintively in their homes. The Poles were fond of them and kept two or three in a cage by the window. Their whistle and call became "one of the saddest sounds of the district. . . . Every spring they seem to be pleading for fresh air and sunlight and freedom for themselves and their friends."

The Baltimore section had four Polish Catholic churches, all crowded at High Mass with men, women, and children. "The congregations are quiet and orderly and neatly dressed; the older women in simple clothing, the younger women and girls in gaudy hats, cheap laces, and jewelry."

In earning their way, Polish immigrants inherited the toughest jobs: in the textile mills of New England, the railroads and lumber mills of the West, the mines of Pennsylvania and West Virginia, the steel mills of Ohio, the slaughterhouses of Chicago, and, later, the automobile plants of Detroit. The women worked in hotels, restaurants, and households as maids and, also, in the sweatshops.

One personal account from the early 1900s describes a day in the life of a factory worker in a Brooklyn, New York, sweatshop. It began at 5:30 A.M. for Sadie Frowne, when she made a cup of coffee and drank it with "a bit of bread" and sometimes fruit. She often arrived at the factory shortly after six, well before the 7:00 A.M. start-up of the machines. Then the boss brought over her allotment of the day's work. Sometimes it was finished by four or five o'clock, sometimes later.

The machines went "like mad all day," run by foot power and leaving the workers "so weak that there is a great temptation to lie right down and sleep." Occasionally, in the rush to keep up with the work, Sadie's finger got caught and the needle went right through it. "It goes so quick, though, that it does not hurt much," she reported. "I bind the finger up with a piece of cotton and go on working. We all have accidents like that."

Two-thirds of the Polish immigrants went to work in the cities and one-third went into farming (particularly in the Midwest, the South, and New England). Those who farmed in New England worked soil that had been tilled to exhaustion and abandoned. But, schooled by harsh farming conditions in Poland, they produced fertile results. Even Calvin Coolidge grudgingly admitted that it took the Polish immigrants to show Yankees how to work the land.

An immigrant inspector at Ellis Island described the way typical Polish immigrants, among whom men outnumbered women two to one, looked. Arriving was a "well-built Pole, with nothing in the world but a carpet bag, a few bundles, and small showing of money. . . . He knows nothing but work. Look at his eyes, mild but good. He has been brought up next to mother earth; turn him loose from the train when he reaches his destination and he will dig. He won't hang around looking for a job, but he will till the soil and before you or I know it he will have crops and that is what he will live on. He comes from a hard country, is tough, and when you and I are going around shivering in an overcoat, he will be going around in his shirt sleeves."

The shock of adjustment was softened by living in Polish-American communities. On one hand, this slowed down Americanization; on the other, *Polonias* bridged the Old and New Worlds. Across that bridge walked second- and third-generation Polish-Americans. The isolation of the newly-arrived immigrants was poignantly described in a 1913 letter to the Massachusetts Immigration Commission. The anonymous letter-writer was in America only four months and still struggling with English. Even so, his strong desire to Americanize and his eloquence break through: "I am polish man. I want be american citizen — and took here first paper in 12 June N 625. But my friends are polish people — I must live with them — I work in the shoes-shop with polish people — I stay all the time with them — at home — in the shop — anywhere. I want live with american people, but I do not know anybody of america. . . . In this way I can live in your country many years — like my friends — and never speak — write well english — and never be good american citizen. . . . If somebody could give me another job between american people, help me live with them and lern english — and could tell me the best way how I can fast lern — it would be very, very good for me. Perhaps you have somebody, here he could help me?"

In a recollection of his experiences in a Polish-American community, a Greek immigrant has written that after six months in America he had neither heard English spoken nor met any Americans. "In the mill there worked Polish men and women and only Polish was spoken in the factory and in the streets of the small town," he wrote. He then quoted his friend: "I believe the captain of our ship made a mistake and instead of bringing us to America brought us to Poland."

For Polish-Americans, the language stakes became very high, touching the very notion of loving one's own mother and father. In effect, it became: love thy parents, learn their language. Father Walvery Jasinski, a spokesman for this viewpoint, has argued that Poles in America studied their native language because they loved and respected their parents: "Only he who values highly what is dear and sacred to his parents loves and respects them. The Polish language is the language they used — and still use — in prayers for the many graces granted to you and to themselves."

As late as the 1940s, the school census in the well-known Polish community of Hamtramck in Detroit showed how the language held on. Instead of a decrease between 1927 and 1945, there was a slight increase in the use of Polish at home. In 1927, 47.7 percent of families with Polish-born fathers used only Polish in the home compared with 49.3 percent in 1945. The rest used a combination of Polish and English at home, except for a scant 1.3 percent in 1927 who used only English. In 1945, *all* families with Polish-born fathers used Polish all or at least part of the time.

Hamtramck residents also checked off many Polish proverbs that they heard or used, particularly:

> What we can delay will not run away.
> Briefly, but concisely.
> Only God is to be believed, not dreams and visions.
> The farther into the forest the more trees there are.
> A guest in the house means God in the home.
> You can tell a master by his boots.
> The pitcher carries water until the handle breaks.
> Hand washes hand.
> He who digs holes under someone else falls into them himself.
> The wise man promises, the fool feels pleased.
> One may do as he pleases in one's own home.

Polish immigrants arrived sensitive to the language issue. At home, following the final 1815 partition of Poland among Russia, Prussia, and Austria, the three overlords had repressed the Polish language. The former two tyrannized and the latter exploited the Poles. Language was the currency of Polish national identity; to threaten it was to arouse the Poles. That is just what the Americanizers did, particularly the Irish-Catholic hierarchy who wanted sermons to be preached in English.

The Polish-language newspaper *Zgoda* spoke out in 1900 on behalf of Polish Catholics who "are greatly opposed" to sermons only in English. It cited the "hard-earned money" contributed by Poles to build churches and schools and quoted the challenge stated by another Polish publication: "We must do our utmost to protect and prolong the life of the Polish Catholic churches." Poles acted on their commitment. In Chicago, for instance, they had by 1920 more parishes than any other ethnic group apart from the Irish.

Feelings ran so strong in favor of Polish religious identity that a splinter group formed the Polish National Catholic Church. In 1904, Father Francis Hodur and 147 lay and clerical representatives established a church that was never large in membership (75,000 in 1960), but reflected the strong emotional ties to Polish identity that existed in an immigrant population that was and is ninety percent Roman Catholic.

"Polish-American" came to mean a combination of commitments held in dynamic equilibrium. At its 1890 meeting, the Polish Roman Catholic Union brought it all together: God, the Old Country, America, and the Polish and English languages. All were treated as part and parcel of Polish-American identity. "After God we value most our nationality and our language: but this does not mean that we are careless about the English language," the resolution stated. "On the contrary, we will take all possible steps to give our children a good foundation and knowledge of the English language and the laws of this country."

Larger, bolder, and older, the Polish National Alliance (PNA) was organized in 1880, though its origins went back to 1842. PNA worked to help Polish immigrants get adjusted and get ahead and to get them naturalized. It ran night schools, offered courses in English and in civics (to answer naturalization questions), provided insurance policies, and generally took up the cudgels for the immigrants. Its annual calendar was a favorite among Polish immigrants, their equivalent of a Farmers' Almanac, filled with encyclopedic information about laws, politics, government, and housekeeping; flavored by wit and wisdom, jokes and humor. Many a Polish family saved these calendars to reread over the years.

In establishing Alliance College in Pennsylvania, PNA confronted a challenge facing all ethnic groups. Immigrant-filled America was not going to save their identity; they had to do it themselves. The country was filled with newcomers from all over the world, strange to it and strange to each other. Each was struggling for his place, each was mixing nostalgia with ambition, each was caught between two worlds.

A commentator writing in 1957 summed up what the Poles realized in 1912 with the opening of Alliance College. American schools "have not given, do not give and will not be able to give our youth" an "understanding and an intelligent love of Poland's history, Polish traditions, and all of Poland's rich culture, past and present."

A Polish immigrant, arriving with a name that was unmanageable to an Anglo-Saxon Ellis Island official, felt the chill immediately. His name was "Americanized," set down on the records in a way that an Anglo-Saxon could handle it, but frequently was only a phonetic echo of the original. This was epitomized in what became a famous political name that originally belonged to a tailor fleeing conscription in the Russian-dominated section of Poland. When he arrived in 1903, Stephen Marciszewski was listed as Muskie, a name his son Edmund would carry into the highest levels of American politics and government, including running for president.

As it actually turned out, the American experience heightened, rather than diluted, Polish nationalism. Many Poles, coming from a partitioned country where they lived isolated in village life, "learned" in America that they were *Poles*. In the Old Country, there were differences in social class and differences between one village and another, but the language and the customs were the same. In America, Polish language and customs separated Poles from other nationalities, who possessed different languages and customs. Fragmented at home, Poles were drawn together in America. They had formed some 4,000 Polish organizations by 1905. (Today, there are an estimated 10,000 Polish fraternal, dramatic, literary, musical, social, cultural, religious, and athletic organizations.)

In America, the Poles celebrated the heroes of the fights for both Polish and American independence. Thaddeus Kosciuszko stood out as a hero in both struggles. When he came to Philadelphia in 1776, a professional engineer who was trained in the military schools of Poland and France, he was appointed colonel of engineers. Thereafter, he played an important part in the American Revolution by fortifying Continental Army positions. At Ticonderoga, Mount Independence, and West Point, and then at Saratoga, his expertise contributed to the victories of the Continental Army. Raised to brigadier-general and made an American citizen, he returned to Poland to fight for the independence of his native country. He failed — but gloriously — in the face of the overpowering forces of Russia and Prussia.

The other Polish political exile who became famous in the American Revolution, Count Casimir Pulaski, died in the defense of Savannah. As organizer and leader of the "Pulaski Legion," he was heralded for the bold cavalry attacks he led and is often called the father of the American cavalry. Both Kosciuszko and Pulaski are still honored by monuments throughout the United States and remembered on special days of celebration, often with parades.

As Polish-Americans developed their communal strength, appeals went out to help their partitioned homeland. Polish nationalism, reminiscent of Irish nationalism, was promoted. The immigrants were rallied to the cause of their homeland in a celebrated article, "The Organization of Poles in America," written in 1879 by a Polish exile, Agaton Giller. He called on Poles in America to support the cause of Polish independence. It was, however, a cause that had to compete with the bread-and-butter efforts of the immigrants. Survival was the main order of sweat-filled weekdays, followed by church on Sunday and feast days.

Meanwhile, as the generations were being sorted out in America, the nightmare of the immigrants about their children haunted *Polonia*. Much of it involved language as well as customs. In the third generation in Hamtramck in the 1950s, a Polish woman whose grandparents came from Galicia told sociologist Wood that she learned to speak English only after she left home and went to work. Her mother, who had been born in northern Michigan, never learned to speak it. She still wore a shawl, "just as my grandmother says they did in Poland." She believed that the people of her Polish rural enclave in Michigan "are different from those of Poland only in one thing: the boys and girls marry for love. The parents don't select the persons they are to marry."

Another Polish girl in Hamtramck reflected the tug and pull of city life on the generations. She cited the "wide breach" between the generations, particularly the third generation which was growing up in the city. For it, English predominated and Polish was used mainly in talking to parents. The public school brought about changes for the Poles as it did for the Italians and other groups. Language became the obvious barometer of change, but at an even deeper and more troubling level, the generations also drifted apart.

What one Polish daughter said represented what so many other sons and daughters felt. While children took on American traits, the parents seemed to "remain unchanged." In describing the tragedy of the situation, she cited the way each "acts according to his own light with the best of intentions, and with the interests of the other often at heart, yet so many times they clash. The tragedy lies in their misunderstanding, neither understands the other, and neither realizes it."

As the centers of *Polonia*, the church and the parish school inevitably moved farther and farther away from the Polish language. At one time Detroit had seven daily programs in Polish over four stations. Only one station was still broadcasting in Polish in 1960. The five Detroit theaters that offered exclusively plays in Polish between 1910 and 1929 are now gone, as are all but one of the city's seven all-Polish newspapers that were being published at the middle of the century. As late as 1930, there were 15 Polish dailies and 64 Polish weeklies, with the daily *Zgoda* of Cleveland selling over 30,000 copies.

Even so, any obituary on Polish identity is altogether premature. The two social scientists who wrote the monumental study *The Polish Peasant in Europe and America* predicted in the 1920s that the third generation in America would abandon the Polish way of life and the fourth generation would be so assimilated as to disappear. But when one of the two, Florian Znaniecki, came to the United States in 1939 he was surprised. Polish identity was still being asserted and pursued. The familiar observation still applied: What the son of an immigrant wishes to forget, the grandson wishes to remember.

There is a case in point from the mid-1970s: best-selling pop singer and song writer Bobby Vinton, whose grandparents came to America at the turn of the century. When he was growing up in Canonsburg, Pennsylvania, he lived in a Polish community, went to Polish schools, "and until I got to high school thought everybody spoke Polish."

In the 1960s, Bobby Vinton became a star, particularly among teenage fans captivated by his romantic ballads. Although he was doing so well with American and European ballads, his repertoire lacked a Polish song. His mother asked him why.

"Ma," he said, "there's no serious Polish songs Americans would understand."

"O.K., write one," she said. "Write one."

The result was "Melody of Love," with several Polish choruses. No major record company would take it, at least at first. When one did, the result was an incredible success and record sales in the millions.

Polish-Americans responded enthusiastically and Bobby Vinton (originally Vintula) found out what social scientists have had some trouble discovering: "I never knew there were so many Polish people. They came to concerts with Polish flags, some wearing national dress. They sing to me in Polish and some even say, 'You know, I was Polish, but I never talked about it until now.' "

7 THE JEWS

The sense of a common fate

I was born in a small town in Russia, and until I was six-
teen I studied in Talmud Torahs and yeshivas, but when
I came to America I changed quickly. I . . . became a
freethinker. . . . But the nature of my feelings is re-
markable. Listen to me: Every year when the month of
Elul rolls around, when the time of Rosh Hashanah and
Yom Kippur approaches, my heart grows heavy and
sad. A melancholy descends on me, a longing gnaws at
my breast. At that time I cannot rest, I wander about
through the streets, lost in thought, depressed. . . .
Where can one hide on Yom Kippur?

In a letter to the editor of the *Jewish Daily Forward* in
1909, an immigrant described his conflict as a Jew in America:
his mind had become secular but his heart was still in the synagogue. He no longer observed the most solemn Jewish holy
days of Rosh Hashanah (the New Year) and Yom Kippur (the
Day of Atonement), but he suffered when he went past a synagogue in New York and heard the cantor chanting the prayers
of the high holy days.

On such occasions, he became "very gloomy" and his depression was so great that he could not "endure" it. "My memory goes back to my happy childhood years. I see clearly before me the small town, the fields, the little pond and the woods around it. . . . My heart is constricted, and I begin to run like a madman till the tears stream from my eyes and then I become calmer."

For the majority of Jewish immigrants, there was no place to hide, no way to run away. Whether or not they went to the synagogue, whether or not they observed religious rituals, whether or not they kept the Sabbath, Judaism was their point of reference. They identified themselves as Jews. When the question of "Who is a Jew?" arose as many broke away from traditional religion, the best answer became "Who is not a Jew?"

In their hearts, Jewish immigrants could not and did not turn from their identity. Nor did non-Jewish Americans let them, particularly when anti-Semitism cast its recurring shadow. Yet, simple labels for that identity, such as race, religion, nation, and culture, fall short of reality. Jewish immigrants came from a score of countries, spoke many languages, represented different cultures, were meticulously observant of their religion, and also consciously indifferent to it.

Even if they did not practice their religion, however, they defined themselves in terms of Judaism. Social scientist Marshall Sklare makes the point succinctly: "A religiously inactive person is thus identified as Jewish by the following rule of thumb: the religion that he does not practice is Judaism rather than Christianity."

Jewish immigrants arrived in America in three waves: a trickle of Sephardic Jews from Spain and Portugal in colonial America; a wave of Ashkenazic German Jews beginning in the late 1840s; and a tidal wave of Russian Jews from eastern Europe beginning in the 1880s. The overwhelming majority of American Jews are traceable to that third wave, which developed as pogroms victimized Russian Jews. Prior to that, there were only a quarter of a million Jews in a U.S. population of fifty million. Between 1881 and 1925, 2.6 million Jewish immigrants came to America from eastern Europe.

One historian of American Jewry has commented that "the Crazy Nihilist who hurled a bomb at Czar Alexander II was the ultimate creator of the New York Ghetto and the man who added 3,000,000 Jews to the American population." That nihilist plot and assassination in 1881 set off a wave of anti-Jewish riots and led to severe repression in Russia and occupied Poland. Persecution of Jews became systematic and ruthless, climaxed by the massacres in the bloody pogroms of 1881-82, 1891, and 1905-06.

Thus the flight of Russian Jews from eastern Europe was a flight from terror, murder, rape, pillaging, and maiming. America was their refuge and the Jews, more than other immigrant groups, brought over entire families, for they could never go home again. For every fifty-six men there were forty-four women among Jewish immigrants; for every three adults one child under fourteen. Nearly seventy percent of these families paid their passage with money lent by relatives. More than half arrived with no money at all. "Their capital was hope," one commentator has noted.

Bringing with them memories of religious persecution, eastern European Jews were sensitive to the threat of anti-Semitism in America. It helped to make them enthusiasts for American freedom and opportunities. This third wave of Jewish immigrants was also linked by the common language of Yiddish, which was derived from medieval High German and included borrowings from Hebrew, Russian, Polish, and English. Their tradition-bound religion was called Orthodox in America and set them apart by strict ritual, observance, and appearance from their Americanized predecessors, the German Jews.

Whatever their background, Jews were linked by what Nathan Glazer and Daniel Moynihan call "the sense of a common fate." They shared a single religion by birth and by tradition and they had the will to be identified as Jews. They faced, as well, the attitude of the non-Jewish world, which reinforced their self-identification.

In America, the Jewish immigrant was pulled between the new and the old. An observer of New York ghetto life, Hutchins Hapgood, who was not Jewish, described the conflict, pointing out that the young immigrant could not forget his origin, yet was attracted by the new world around him. On one hand, there was a nature "at once religious and susceptible," with "a deep love for his race and the old things"; on the other existed a nature "keenly sensitive to the charm of this American environment, with its practical and national opportunities."

Jewish immigrants were, therefore, a bundle of contradictions. They shared the twin drives of faith and hope with all other immigrant groups, but probably felt the contradictions of American immigrant life more than most. They were both idealistic and materialistic. They believed that man should reach for the stars and uphold the highest standards, but also in being practical and having a strategy for coping with the real world. Many were liberal in politics but conservative in religion. They excelled in both business and arts, were tough-minded and soft-hearted. They had a passionate commitment to learning. (It was not for nothing that their sacred book of Scriptural commentary, the Talmud, described them as "the people of the book.") But they also were passionate about wages, about profits, and about success. Author Harvey Swados, on a nostalgic visit to the Lower East Side, noted that the Jewish immigrant had "a frenzied mania to make it in America."

The double-edged Jewish response to America was poignantly recalled by an immigrant named Ephraim E. Lisitzky. The time and place were Boston in about 1900 and he was alone in the synagogue, "swaying over the open Talmud, chanting in the old country tone." Suddenly he heard loud sounds from the street. They were "the sounds of the new life in which I have been cast and out of whose turmoil I have fled into this desolate haven. The cries reproached me mockingly! What are you doing among us, you unworldly idler?''

His own father was a peddler by day and by night. By day, he peddled rags and bottles; by night it was copies of Hebrew lessons to prepare young Jews for their Bar Mitzvah, the ritual celebrating arrival at the age of responsibility. The determination and the pain of "making it" for those first Jewish immigrants are reflected in the picture of the father as peddler:

> He walked his route through the city, crying: "R-r-rags and bottles!" He looked up to the tenement houses, looking at the windows for a sign that one of the tenants wanted to bargain over their discards and rags. Sometimes young rowdies threw stones at him, and in the winter snowballs with pieces of coal inside, sometimes hoodlums pulled his beard, sometimes he'd be attacked in dark hallways and his pockets emptied. "Rags and bottles!" he would call again after such a mishap, his voice ringing with pain and grief, but not with bitterness or protest. He was inured to suffering and submitted to it.

As a route followed by many Jewish immigrants, peddling led to comfort, affluence, and, for some, eventually great wealth. It led from tenement to duplex, from ghetto to country club, from pushcart to golf cart. It made sense as a starting point because it offered an opportunity to learn the language and ways of America and also enabled the immigrant to take off from work on the Sabbath and on holy days. It offered a chance to blend the old and the new.

For Russian Jews, buying and selling was already a habit imposed by the Czar. In the nineteenth century Russian Jews were confined to an area known as the Pale of Settlement in western and southwestern Russia and in the provinces of occupied Poland. Excluded from owning land, they became traders, merchants, and artisans, middlemen between the nobility and the oppressed peasantry. Nearly three-fourths were

engaged in petty commerce and industry. They were the peddlers, petty retailers, and moneylenders.

Unsuited to farming and with half of them lacking any
trade, Jewish immigrants settled in the cities and gravitated
toward peddling. When they went West it was to sell clothing,
notions, and all sorts of merchandise to the people of the frontier and eventually to settle down and open shops. On these
foundations they established the large clothing establishments
and department stores that now flourish across the country.

The American Jewish experience was epitomized on New
York's Lower East Side, which extended from the southern tip
of Manhattan to Houston Street. It was the largest concentration of American Jews, their "capital." New York has remained so. Well past the middle of this century, about half of
the country's Jews were living in New York City and its suburbs and practically every other Jew in America had a link to
New York — having once lived there or having relatives who
did.

A million Jews crowded into the Lower East Side ghetto, a
place of staggering crowds, teeming tenements, and hectic
street markets. Only Bombay had a denser population. Ann
Novotny, who has chronicled the immigrant experience, describes the main market as a place "where unbelievable
numbers of men and women shouted at each other in a dozen
languages, as they jostled their way around pushcarts piled
with merchandise. . . . There were piles of fish, meats, chick-
en, ripe cheeses, fruit, pickles, and huge loaves of black bread.
Interspersed between the food stalls were other carts laden
with glasses and tinware, remnants of lace and carpeting,
boots, stockings for six cents a pair, and children's underwear
for a nickel." Pushcart vendors shouted, shopkeepers tried to
buttonhole people on the street, peddlers on foot hawked their
wares. Turn-of-the-century photographs show that it was hard
even to walk through the seething mass of humanity.

As they nearly suffocated in their tenements, the immigrants also sweated in the shops where they worked. A lead-

ing Yiddish writer, Z. Libin, recalled: "My muse was born in the dark sweat shop, her first painful cry resounded near the Singer machine, she was brought up in the tenement tombs." In the infamous sweatshop, the hours were long, the pay scandalously low, the working conditions "foul in the extreme" (as one official report stated in 1887).

The immigrants worked in factories, did staggering amounts of piecework at home for contractors, or slaved in tenement apartments that had been converted into shops. Where apartments were used, the sewing machine operators, basters, and finishers worked in the "front room"; the irons were heated in the kitchen where the pressers labored. A U.S. government report described immigrant workers living and working together "in large numbers, in a few small, foul, ill-smelling rooms, without ventilation, water, or nearby toilets." The immigrants "slept on the unswept floors littered with the work, the work table serving as the dining table as well." A social worker in New York found that some tailors rented a single room where they worked in one corner and rented out seats in the rest of the room at 37 cents for each man wanting to work there. (It cost 50 cents for a man assisted by a girl.)

The flood of immigrants kept sweatshop operators supplied with labor. In New York, newcomers flocked to the "labor exchange" on Essex near Hester Street, which was bitterly labeled the *Chazer Mark* ("Pig Market"). There, newcomers were recruited into the sweatshop system of the clothing trade, which attracted the large number of Russian Jews who already had the necessary skills. Of 400,000 Jewish immigrants who arrived with trades between 1899 and 1910, half were tailors (145,000) or dressmakers or had skills such as hat maker or furrier.

What stood out in this ghetto life in New York — as well as in its smaller versions in such cities as Boston, Chicago, and Philadelphia — was the "frenzied mania to make it in America." The ghetto was not a place to which the immigrants surrendered, but one from which they struggled to escape. In the

Old World, Jews were crowded into village *shtetls,* such as the one in the Broadway musical *Fiddler on the Roof,* where they lived apart in a beehive of ramshackle huts and mud streets. The *shtetl,* as James Yaffe notes, "was a place to live in"; the Lower East Side "was a place to leave."

And leave they did, propelled by their energy, their intelligence, and their hard work. Their qualifications and their qualities suited an American economy in which the need for farmers and manual workers was declining. There were opportunities for traders and for businessmen ready to enter newly-developing industries. Thrift, sobriety, and ambition were being highly rewarded, and these were the traits that distinguished Jewish immigrants. Education was a major road upward. For the Jews this meant a natural transfer of their zeal for Talmudic learning to a zeal for secular learning. Glazer and Moynihan have aptly noted that they had "a passion for education that was unique in American history."

The children of the ghetto were passionate pupils in the public schools, responding energetically to the expanded opportunities to be found in America. Education was a route up and out of the ghetto. A famous photograph from the early 1900s shows Jewish children lined up all the way around the block as they waited for the local branch of the public library to open. After school, at three o'clock, ghetto children by the hundreds went to the local branch of the public library to do their homework and to get help from the librarian in selecting books. *Uncle Tom's Cabin* and biblical stories were among their favorites. At one branch, a thousand English books a day were being borrowed.

As immigrant children grew older, there were free classes at the Educational Alliance or at Cooper Union, where it was possible to study engineering and art. Or else they could attend one of New York's free colleges, such as the celebrated "Harvard" of New York's Jewish immigrant families, the City College of New York (CCNY). Professor Paul Weiss of Yale University, now retired, has recalled his own CCNY days in which "eighty percent of the students were Jewish, from poor Orthodox families. We were noisy, talkative, anxious to learn, full of excitement. We devoured all the books that were assigned to us, and then grabbed for more. And we never stopped discussing, debating — let's face it, yelling about what we were learning. What a racket there was in the lunchroom!"

As early as 1907, a New York Italian newspaper was bluntly urging its readers: "Let us do as the Jews do." Which meant, "invade the schools, teach ourselves, have our children taught." The newspaper's editorial cited "the giant strides" of Jewish immigrants. They are "the lawyers, judges, doctors, professors, teachers, managers of theatres, monopolists of the arts. The most perfect institutions of mutual aid and providence are Israelite. Their clubs, social, political, artistic, and professional, are the best of their kind. The schools are the most frequented and active."

Accounts of Jewish ghetto life overflow with descriptions of its vitality. Eastern European Jews founded synagogue after synagogue. Size did not matter; it took only ten Jews from the same town to form one. Almost as soon as they arrived, immigrants were on the streets peddling goods and maneuvering pushcarts from street to alley to sidewalk, while their children ran errands, played, or hurried off to Hebrew school. Coffee shops sprang up in which the air was filled with cigarette smoke and polemics. The rhythm of life ebbed and flowed with family parties to celebrate engagements and weddings and with solemn gatherings to mark the holy days.

The immigrants "all lived together, if not in harmony, then at least in a sense of common participation in the vitality of their district and that era," writes humorist Harry Golden, who grew up on the Lower East Side. He paints a picture of a ghetto tenement scene: "The crotchety maiden aunt, Grandmother and Grandfather, the wild-eyed high school boy who had just begun to study Marx, Uncle Boris from uptown and the boarder who studied Spinoza and Shakespeare until late at night every night — all sat at the same table and shared the same bread, soup, and potatoes. They also got involved in many-sided conversations and debates."

In a 1906 report on Jewish immigrants, the observers noted that as their number in a district "increases the number of 'gin mills' decreases." Instead, there were "coffee and cake parlors" that often became restaurants, but particularly "coffee saloons." Actually, the coffee houses served mainly tea *a la Russe* — with a slice of lemon — and were, in effect, workingmen's clubs. The clientele was made up of regulars and the personality of the proprietor shaped the atmosphere, whether it was political, theatrical, or artistic. Those who agreed with the proprietor's opinions or his interests came to his coffee house — socialists to socialist coffee houses, music lovers to theirs, "chess-cranks" to theirs. The latter went to what were considered quiet coffee houses, the "philosophers" to those where things were "oracular and demonstrative."

Yiddish theatres also flourished. In the early 1900s on the Lower East Side, when five of them were offering performances seven days a week plus matinees on Saturday and Sunday, an estimated five to seven thousand turned out every night. The largest theatre was the equal of the largest theatre serving New York's non-Jewish theatregoers. In those days, it was not the play so much as the stars that were the thing, particularly Jacob P. Adler and Bertha Kalisch. (One critic claimed she was "as good as Sarah Bernhardt at Sarah's best, but never as bad as Sarah at Sarah's worst.") After Maurice Schwartz founded the Yiddish Art Theatre in 1918, Yiddish theatre attracted attention outside the Jewish community and produced such stars as Molly Picon and Muni Weisenfreund (Paul Muni).

Jewish humor provided a characteristic way of dealing with the harsh realities of life. It mixed optimism and pessimism and the jokes seemed to be on the Jews themselves — until, that is, a closer look showed the philosophic twist, the perceptive thrust toward the truth, the coming to terms with a problem. Harry Golden, himself a rich source of Jewish humor, describes it as "the sure cure for the doldrums, the blues, the fits of melancholia and depression" that plague the middle class today. In all his years on the Lower East Side, he never saw anyone take a tranquilizer or a sleeping pill, but he "heard jokes and wisecracks all day long from the breakfast table until late at night."

From Sholom Aleichem to the Marx Brothers and on to Jack Benny, Milton Berle, Sid Caesar, Danny Kaye, Mel Brooks, and Neil Simon, Jewish humor has become a national pastime on stage, screen, radio, and television. The funny story, the witty comeback, and the humorous routine abound. So-called Jewish humor also distinguishes the Jewish intellectual who can switch from the abstract to the concrete by telling an amusing story, often with a punch line in Yiddish. As they worked their way out of the ghettos, the Jews brought along their bittersweet laughter.

For an ambitious young immigrant, for whom many doors to opportunity were closed, there was no business like show business. Jewish success stories thus abounded in the entertainment field, including those of Israel Baline of Temun, Siberia; Samuel Goldfish of Warsaw, Poland; and Solomon Hurok of Pogar in the southern Ukraine.

Israel Baline was only four years old when his father, a rabbi, took him and his seven brothers and sisters to America following a Russian pogrom. They left when their home was burned and arrived on the Lower East Side in 1893. Israel worked as a newsboy and as a singing waiter until he got a job with a music publisher in 1909 and launched his songwriting career as Irving Berlin. A thousand popular songs later, he was said to have earned more money from his work than any other composer in history. His hits included *Alexander's Ragtime Band, White Christmas,* and, appropriately, *God Bless America.*

Samuel Goldfish ran away from home in 1894 at the age of eleven and arrived at Ellis Island two years later. He got his first job at three dollars a week. When he became a citizen in 1902, he changed his name to Samuel Goldwyn, a name that would become world-famous in movie-making. He was in the company of what motion picture historian Gerald Mast has called "a very specific breed of businessmen" who were either Jewish immigrants or sons of Jewish immigrants. They came into the movie industry by following their bent for business, moving into amusement parks, penny arcades, and nickelodeons, then into movies. "Such was the series of small steps that a Goldwyn (né Goldfish) or (Adolph) Zukor or (Lewis J.) Selznick took from the Jewish ghetto to multimillion-dollar arbiter of national artistic tastes," Mast writes.

Solomon Hurok arrived in 1906 with less than three rubles in his pocket and went first to live in Philadelphia where he sold sewing needles, drove streetcars, washed soda bottles, and bundled newspapers. Moving to New York, he worked in a hardware store and went to night classes at the Educational Alliance to improve his English, meanwhile attending every concert he could afford. He began by organizing musical events for local groups and soon — by the age of twenty-one — was renting Madison Square Garden. Over a span of more than fifty years, Sol Hurok became *the* impressario of concerts and ballets in the United States.

The dark side of the Jewish experience in America was the anti-Semitism that spread as the number of Jewish immigrants increased. The symbolic date is 1877, when the German-Jewish banker Joseph Seligman and his family were turned away at a resort hotel in Saratoga Springs, New York. A so-called gentleman's agreement operated, excluding Jews from country clubs, fraternities, and business groups, and limiting their admission to prestige colleges and professional schools. For refugees from pogroms, the Old World was thus echoed in the New.

Anti-Semitism focused on the eastern European Jews. They stood out. The German Jews were regarded as Germans who happened to be Jews, while the new immigrants were

Jews who happened to be from eastern Europe. Arriving as impoverished and undernourished refugees, they wore long black coats and long untamed beards, spoke Yiddish, and practiced distinctive religious rituals.

As it did other immigrant groups, the press criticized them. The *New York Tribune* reported in 1882 that "numerous complaints have been made in regard to the Hebrew immigrants who lounge about Battery Park." In addition, the Jews suffered from the traditional Shylock stereotype and the disdain that native Americans felt toward peddlers. Even the crusading journalist Jacob Riis subscribed to the stereotype by saying of Russian Jews that "money is their God."

As a historian of American nativism, John Higham, notes, the Russian Jews suffered for their economic success. Having "a dynamism rare among foreign groups," they faced sharpened discrimination partly as the result of their "swift upward thrust." Higham adds that the Jews "met the most economic discrimination" among the "new" immigrants of the late nineteenth and early twentieth century.

Within the American Jewish community, the more Americanized German Jews felt uncomfortable with the foreign-looking eastern European Jews. In line with the Jewish belief in education as the solution to problems, German Jews organized educational programs, such as the Educational Alliance in New York, which provided Americanizing courses in civics, English, engineering, and various practical subjects. Settlement houses were established and social and athletic facilities made available. Although the German Jew wanted to shake off vestiges of the Old World, the Russian Jew had strong ties to tradition. He put down the Americanized Jew as an "allrightnik."

The conflict over Americanization centered on religion. As a result, American Judaism developed three major branches: Orthodox, Reform, and Conservative. The major figure of the modernizing Reform movement was a mid-nineteenth-century immigrant rabbi, Isaac Mayer Wise, who was active until his death in 1900. As the Reform movement gained strength among German Jews, Rabbi Wise made his theme clear: "The Hebrew is Americanized and his religion is naturalized, they are no longer strangers, and they are perfectly at home in this blessed country."

To the tradition-minded newcomers from eastern Europe, however, the reformers were becoming a "Jewish Protestant Church." For them, the Reform way constituted Americanization in the style of the assimilated, affluent, and condescending German Jews. They viewed it as rejection of the religious way of life that had nurtured them in eastern Europe and most did not want to go that far.

A third way emerged, the Conservative Movement, which centered about New York's Jewish Theological Seminary which was founded in 1886. It occupied a middle ground between the Orthodox, who were committed to unchanging tradition, and the Reform, who believed in changing tradition. All three parts of American Judaism developed along parallel lines, with their own viewpoint, organization, and leadership.

In all three branches of Judaism, the rabbi occupied a special place. Unlike the priest or minister who performs sacramental functions, the rabbi serves as what the word itself means — he is a "teacher," which by extension means scholar, and therefore confers personal distinction in the Jewish community. To the sons of the eastern European immigrants who achieved success in business and prestige in the professions, another group was added: those who became rabbis.

Whatever his branch of Judaism, which also included various offshoots, the rabbi contributed to the wholeness of the Jewish community. Inside that community, there were debates, polemics, controversy, and competition. But there also was a unifying element, what social scientist Louis Wirth called the "ability to act corporately." In his monumental 1928 study of Jewish ghetto life, Wirth cited the "common set of attitudes and values based upon common traditions, similar experience, and common problems."

What emerged from the Jewish immigrant experience was "the greatest collective Horatio Alger story in American immigration history," as social scientist Milton M. Gordon observed from the vantage point of the 1960s. It was a collective success expressed in personal terms, for the immigrants and their children counted their blessings. One immigrant, for instance, wrote to the *Jewish Daily Forward* in 1956, raising a question about the "good old days." Were they really that good? "The truth is that those times were not so good," he said. "I still remember my home town in Russia, our simple little house lighted at night by a small kerosene lamp, the door thatched with straw nailed down with sackcloth to keep it warm in winter. I still remember the mud in the steets of the town, so deep it was difficult to get around; our fear of the Gentiles; and who can forget the poverty — the times when there wasn't even a crust of bread?"

Nor were the "good old days" so great at the beginning in America. The immigrant also recalled that he had lived on New York's East Side in a tenement "and had to climb to the fourth and fifth floors to tiny rooms that were dark and airless. There were no bathrooms in the flats. A large bathtub stood in the kitchen near the old iron stove that was heated with coal in which mothers also did the laundry." He remembered working in the shops fourteen and sixteen hours a day, six days a week.

When he considered the modern conveniences, achievements, and opportunities, he saw that "there's nothing to be nostalgic about. I say we now have the good times and we do not have to long for the past."

The *Jewish Daily Forward,* organ of New York's Yiddish-speaking population since 1897, agreed: "The little town with its mud, the poor hut with the kerosene lamp, the bitter life in Czarist Russia, and the old-time sweatshops here, contrast dramatically with today's comfortable life in our country. It's like the difference between day and night." In America, Jewish immigrants could rejoice in their "common fate."

8

AND SO MANY OTHERS

From all corners of the world

For if, when the roar of the day's work has subsided, you watch the men, women, and children that pour out of factories, shops, and mills; the Germans and Irish and Scotch, the Swedes, Norwegians, Poles, and Jews, Bohemians, Slovaks, Italians, Greeks; if you follow the human tides to the great foreign quarters of the city, you may be amazed at the scenes you will suddenly enter; opening scenes in a slow but irresistible process, which has for its raw material all the old peoples of Europe. . . . The Tower of Babel's drama reversed. Chicago a mixing bowl for the nations.

One may find for the asking an Italian, a German, a French, African, Spanish, Bohemian, Russian, Scandinavian, Jewish, and Chinese colony. Even the Arab, who peddles "holy earth" from the Battery as a direct importation from Jerusalem, has his exclusive preserves at the lower end of Washington Street. The one thing you shall vainly ask for in the chief city of America is a distinctively American community.

What was evident in Chicago and New York was evident in

all American cities at the turn of this century: an incredible spectacle of humanity in its many national varieties. The Chicago description was written in 1910 by a well-known author of the time, Ernest Poole. The New York one was by the celebrated journalist Jacob Riis. Each was depicting the phenomenon summed up by Ralph Waldo Emerson: "a heterogeneous population crowding in on ships from all corners of the world to the great gates of North America."

With the "new" immigration of the late nineteenth and early twentieth century, the newcomers created an ethnic mosaic that still survives in its richness. Besides the arriving millions of Italians, Poles, and Jews, there were Serbs, Croats, Slovenes, Montenegrins, Moravians, Dalmatians, Ukrainians, Ruthenians, Magyars, Bulgarians, Lithuanians, Latvians, Estonians, Albanians, Roumanians, Portuguese, Spanish, and Greeks. From the eastern Mediterranean, Armenians, Syrians, and Lebanese came to escape Turkish misrule and oppression. (One historian reports that the first picture sent back of a Syrian family in America was taken with a placard which read "The children and I have happily found liberty.") Meanwhile, on the West Coast, 300,000 Chinese had arrived between 1850 and 1882.

Beginning with their first Ellis Island experience, the various nationalities were thrust into close contact with each other. A fifteen-year-old arrival named Louis Adamic, who later became a prominent journalist and writer on immigrant affairs, recalled his first night in America, which was spent sleeping on Ellis Island along with hundreds of other new arrivals in an immense hall containing tiers of narrow bunks. Below him was "a Turk who slept with his turban round his head." Adamic, who came in 1913 from a village called Blato in Slovenia, which was part of Austria and is now in Yugoslavia, recalled thinking how "curious" it was to be spending "a night in such close proximity to a Turk, for Turks were traditional enemies of Balkan peoples, including my own nation."

Each immigrant group was determined to assert its unique

identity, particularly when it had experienced repression in the Old Country. America was the place where they freed themselves of alien oppression and they responded to the free atmosphere. In Europe, people of the same language, culture, and religion were separated by political borders; in America, they could reunite.

But America, beginning at Ellis Island, did not see them as clearly as they saw themselves. From Russia came both Russians and Jews; from countries dominated by the Czar came Poles, Latvians, Finns, and Lithuanians. From Turkish control came the Syrians and Lebanese and Armenians. To list the latter under the category of Turkish immigrants was not only a mistake, it was an insult!

Nor could the Slavs be lumped together. Besides the Poles, the West Slavs included the Slovaks and Czechs or Bohemians. The South Slavs included Serbs, Croats, Slovenes, Macedonians, Montenegrins, and Bosnians. The Ukrainians were categorized as East Slavs.

Immigrant spokesmen urged their countrymen to stand up and be counted and to impress upon Americans that, for instance, a Lithuanian was not a Pole or a Russian. All may have lived under the heel of the Czar, but that was a result of force, not choice. In 1896 one Chicago Lithuanian paper urged its readers to identify themselves as Lithuanians "always and everywhere." It asserted the ethnic pride that distinguished each immigrant group: "He who denies his own nationality and tries to assimilate with another nationality will not be respected by the people of that nationality. Lithuanians, do not conceal your Lithuanianism, because Lithuania in her past was one of the most honorable nations among the European nations. Now it is our duty, by our own good conduct, to regain the lost honor of our nation. Let us honor ourselves; then others will respect us."

For all the variety, the prevailing two ingredients of faith and hope persisted. Worsening economic conditions had pushed immigrants from all over Europe toward the magnetic opportunities of America. A typical immigrant wrote to a young brother in a small Dalmatian village near the Adriatic Sea, explaining that the price of homesickness was worth the rewards in America. He missed his family as well as "the joyful Sunday activities in our village, particularly the morning chat sessions in front of our church, the afternoon unions of the men in the harbor tavern, and the evening folk dances in the village courtyard" as well as many other things "which seemed so important in my life over there." He was "willing to sacrifice much of what I had at home for the new life that has become mine in America." He had "a good job," new friends, new pastimes, money in the bank, and "already have enough saved for your passage if you should change your mind about coming to this country." Such letters to the Old Country continued to lure immigrants from every part of Europe.

A Croatian writer and politician who sailed to America to visit Croatian colonies noticed entire Croatian families on board ship. When he asked why they were leaving their homeland, he found that it was an "unnecessary question." "Misery. There is no money to pay the taxes. Children and old people are starving at home. No income, no jobs." Another observer was told by Croatians who were emigrating to America: "We are going to find out whether there is still justice in the world."

Since their religious faith was important in holding on to their identity, parishes were formed as ethnic enclaves. The immigrants wanted native priests and freedom from domination by Irish-Catholic clergy. If they came over as members of Protestant and Orthodox churches, they were determined to uphold their particular denomination.

A 1910 breakdown of church affiliations among Slavic immigrants showed how they gravitated toward their own kind. The Bohemians were overwhelmingly Catholics and most remained so in the United States, though 15 to 20 percent were classed as "free thinkers." By 1910, they had organized 166 Catholic parishes and a scattering of Protestant churches, ranging from Presbyterian to Baptist. The Slovaks not only had 110 churches for their majority Catholic affiliation, but a considerable number of United Greek Catholic churches and 10 Greek Orthodox and 51 Protestant churches. The Ruthenians (from the Ukraine) had 80 United Greek Catholic, 26 Greek Orthodox, and two Protestant churches. The Slovenians were practically all in an estimated 20 Catholic parishes, while the Russians were in some 50 Orthodox churches.

As historian Carl Wittke points out in his classic study of the immigrants, "for most groups, the immigrants' church has been probably the strongest single force in preserving" their solidarity. Thus America experienced religious variety to match ethnic variety. Colorful customs, rituals, and religious festivals — as well as the rise of distinctive styles of church architecture — enriched both the urban and rural scene.

On the hard road to Americanization, the various immigrant groups experienced their own version of the struggle to get established. Making a living was the focus of their energies and they needed all the moral support they could get. A Ruthenian Greek-Catholic priest, Father Paul Tymkevich, commented on what his countrymen faced as he helped them: "My people do not live in America, they live underneath America. America goes on over their heads. America does not begin till a man is a workingman, till he is earning two dollars a day."

A Greek traveling through the western United States noted in a 1911 *Greek-American Guide* that one of his countrymen was bound to feel "grief and sorrow" in seeing "at nearly every mile of railway little groups of his own people with pick and shovel in their hands." They had left their "beloved fatherland" and were building and repairing railroads "in the hope of acquiring a few thousand francs — instead of which they acquire rheumatism, tuberculosis, venereal diseases, and those other ills, while others are deprived of feet, hands, eyes, and some their lives!" Another writer described the Greek immigrant scraping along "on small pay and hard work in the foul factory air — so different from the free hillsides of Hellas — and the fouler air of the tenement where he is obliged to herd."

Slavic immigrants sweated in the mines and the factories of the country, forced to earn their way in backbreaking and dangerous jobs. They worked in coal and coke, iron and steel. They worked on construction gangs that "laid the steel . . . from ocean to ocean" and their graves were "marked by the telegraph poles," or were found in the clothing sweatshops of Chicago and the cigar-making sweatshops of New York.

Early in the century, a social worker described the incredible energy of Bohemian mothers who worked in cigar factories: "Besides the factory work they have the bearing and rearing of children, and sewing, cooking, washing, and cleaning to do in their homes." On a Bohemian block in New York, everyone was asleep by 9:00 P.M. during winter, since the working day began at 5:30 in the morning. "The Bohemians are cut off from the life of the city," the social worker reported, "partly by their inability to speak English, and partly by their being so overworked that they have no time even to see what other people are doing."

One group in particular went into peddling: the Christian immigrants from Lebanon and Syria. A former U.S. Commissioner of Immigration, Edward Corsi, described their arrival in "red fezzes, short open jackets, short baggy blue trousers to the calves and ill-fitting shoes." He claimed that from his first day in America such a Levantine immigrant would be on the street peddling and "would have added five dollars to his hoard, while the Irish or German immigrant would be bustling about trying to find work to enable him to earn a dollar."

Because the people of the "new" immigration seemed so alien to native Americans, possessed such a different appearance, custom, and style, and were primarily impoverished peasants, they faced hostility and discrimination. A cry went up to restrict their numbers. It came not only from working people who worried about their jobs whenever the economy slumped, but also from intellectual circles, including Harvard academics.

A typical argument against immigrants from southeastern Europe was propounded by Nathaniel Shaler of the Laurence Scientific School at Harvard. In a particularly influential article published in the *Atlantic Monthly* in 1893, he contended that the European peasant "knows himself to be by birthright a member of an inferior class, from which there is practically no chance of escaping. He is in essentially the same state as the Southern Negro." The observation was ironic, to say the least, for similar remarks originally had been made about the Irish, who by the end of the nineteenth century were assuming a prominent role in American life. An Irishman writing home in 1851 quoted an American black as saying: "My master is a great tyrant. He treats me as badly as if I was a common Irishman."

The theme that ran through most of the hostility toward the "new" immigrants was that they would impoverish rather than enrich America and endanger rather than strengthen the republic. Like others in favor of restricted immigration, Shaler warned of "the gravity of the danger which the mass of European immigration brings to us." That argument was pushed for forty years, until in the 1920s the United States passed laws unfairly restricting immigration by the "new" immigrants. By that time, however, when the Golden Door was no longer wide open, the immigrants had arrived by the millions and were enriching, strengthening, and changing America.

They were proving themselves as they always had: at the price of prodigious effort and in the face of extreme hardship. Since it was the Irish who set the example of group unity and ethnic militancy, it is appropriate to quote an Irishman, George F. Mulligan, and his advice to the Greek Achaian League of Chicago. In a 1910 speech, Mulligan set down the formula that new and old immigrants had to follow — and did. They must organize and unite, Mulligan advised: "You all

111

know how easy it is to take one slender stick in the hands and break it with little effort; but take a hundred sticks bound together tightly and no man can break them."

The various new immigrant groups were already binding themselves together. Their first efforts were mutual aid and social events. Beginning in the late nineteenth century, Slavic publications were filled with reports of the activities of aid societies, concerts, dances, picnics, and sporting events. Many "wife wanted" — as well as "help wanted" — advertisements appeared. Whereas the Czechs tended to come over in family units, many Slovaks were "birds of passage" who planned to return home.

Among all the groups, the Bohemians were perhaps the best organized in terms of social, fraternal, and protective societies. In Chicago alone, they had 228 building and loan associations by 1915. Their immigration reached its peak in 1907 (there were 40,000 in America in 1870), but their oldest fraternal organization dated back to 1854. In addition, the *Sòkol* of the Bohemians paralleled the German *Turnverein*, holding giant gymnastic exhibitions at regular intervals.

In 1891, with the beginning of the large Greek immigration, Prince George, the second son of the Greek king, toured the United States and urged leading Greeks in New York City to form an organization. The Hellenic Brotherhood of Athens was established and set about recruiting a priest from Greece. In Chicago, the "Therapnean" was doing the same. From these beginnings came the Orthodox Greek communities in the United States. As Greek immigration increased, reaching a peak of 300,000 in the decade before World War I, it spread to 130 communities, where the immigrants usually organized themselves, elected officers, and obtained a Greek Orthodox priest. In the "Little Greece" areas of cities like Detroit, St. Louis, Akron, and Chicago, the flavor was authentically Hellenic, from the shops to the street signs, from the coffee houses to the Greek games that children played on the streets.

Among the Greeks, as among the other immigrant groups,

newspapers and magazines proliferated. By 1904 there were two Greek daily newspapers in New York; by 1913 there were 14 Greek weeklies in the United States. The first Armenian newspaper dated back to 1888 and the Croatians had their first newspaper in 1891. The first and most distinguished Arabic newspaper in America, *Al-Hoda* ("The Guidance"), was launched in 1898 in Philadelphia and in 1903 became a daily in New York, which had the largest concentration of Syrian and Lebanese immigrants.

"New" and "old" immigration created a virtual Babel of newspapers in the United States. In the peak year of 1914 there were 1,300 foreign-language newspapers and periodicals. There were 140 dailies (one-third in German). New York alone had 32 foreign-language dailies, including ten in German, five in Yiddish, three in Italian, two each in Arabic, Bohemian, and Greek, and one each in Chinese, Croatian, French, Hungarian, Russian, Serbian, Slovakian, and Slovenian.

The foreign-language newspapers and the mutual aid societies helped the immigrants to sink their new roots. They were experiencing the personal transition between two worlds. They were not of the Old Country any more, but also not fully of the new one. As one Croatian immigrant commented: "We are somewhere between the earth and the skies and we feel that we are no longer immigrants as we used to be; now we are a special class, alienated from the homeland and not accustomed to this new world."

The first sign was in the way their clothing changed. Actually, this happened to many as soon as the ferry from Ellis Island landed at Battery Park. Often, relatives were waiting with "American" clothing so they wouldn't be embarrassed by bringing "greenhorns" into the neighborhood. They dragged their relatives into public dressing rooms and made them change their clothing on the spot. "Half an hour after the ferry from Ellis Island had unloaded a fresh crowd of immigrants," Ann Novotny has written, "the public dressing rooms and even the sidewalks around the park were littered with abandoned kerchiefs, visored caps, and occasional shirts and trousers."

One elderly Roumanian immigrant complained: "I do not recognize my countrymen. They look just like others and unless I hear them talk our language, I think they are Poles or Serbs or Irish. The men have even clipped their moustaches, the sign of virile manhood. But such is the fashion here. With their smooth faces men look like women, just as the women with their bobbed hair try to look boyish. It is the world upside down. I cannot understand how they are able to do these things and still claim that they are Roumanians."

After the change in clothing came the changes in Old World customs, changes that were much harder on older, more ingrained immigrants. "Nowadays everything goes fast," sighed an elderly woman. "Christenings are done within a twinkle of the eye. The priests are rushing so much in saying their prayers that I fear the evil spirit does not have the time to depart from the child, before the sacrament of the Holy Spirit takes place. . . . The wedding festivities are shortened to one day. Who can afford to be merry for three days! The factory closes its doors to you if you are late 15 minutes."

In Akron, Ohio, an immigrant Roumanian woman lamented the pressures of American life upon religious customs, while at the same testifying to the strong hold such customs still had not only upon her but upon all immigrants:

Saints' days! They are all the same for the people here. The factories are closed on Labor Day but we must work on St. George's Day, on the Holy Assumption and on St. Elias' Day, to speak nothing of all the other Fêtes. Wouldn't the lightning strike us if we dared do that in our Country? There we all used to go to church, but here we go to the factory instead. However I never neglect to light my oil lamp before the holy icons. In this way my conscience is at ease with the Saints. Sometimes I think I am getting to be a heathen. But then I see so many churches here and so many different ways of being a Christian that I say: well! those people who have more learning than myself must

114

know better, when they work on Saints' days instead of going to church.

But a religious focus was far from lost when religious customs were modified. Among the Roumanians, the idea of a band at a funeral, especially when a young person died, was being abandoned, as was the custom of putting a coin in the hand of the deceased. (The coin was supposed to pay his passage to St. Peter.) But "Colindatorii" (carol singers) still went from one Roumanian home to another singing "Good morning, old Christmas Eve" and collecting coins for the church. In Greek households, religious icons were on display, particularly of the country's patron saint, St. George, slaying the dragon, and in many households a little lamp was lighted in front of the icon every Saturday night and on the eve of holy days. In their reports of visits to immigrant homes, social workers and journalists invariably reported seeing religious pictures on the walls. One memorable old photograph taken of a Lithuanian immigrant living in one room shows him seated in front of a wall covered with gilt-framed religious pictures: a private shrine enhancing his cramped world in an American tenement.

If changes in clothing and in religious customs were signs of Americanization among the immigrants, it was the drift away from the Old Country language that was even more striking among their children. Their encounter with the many other immigrant strands in America took place, of course, primarily in the public schools. One vivid 1903 report on a New York school at Catherine and Henry Streets illustrates the mixing of the nationalities. The school children came from separate ethnic neighborhoods, but in that single school more than twenty-five nationalities were represented, including Swedes, Austrians, Greeks, Russians, English, Irish, Scotch, Welsh, Roumanians, Italians, Poles, Hungarians, Canadians, Armenians, Germans, and Chinese.

Each immigrant and each child of an immigrant was living

115

out a personal merger of the old and the new. America thus became a stage for millions of individual dramas whose plots revolved around the Old Country and the New. In a moving conclusion to his study of the immigrant experience, historian Oscar Handlin describes an imaginary conversation between an immigrant father and son in which both the meaning of America and the meaning of emigration to America emerge.

The father had been uprooted and could "no longer recede into the warm obscurity where like and like and like conceal the one's identity." Through the pain of separation, something beautiful had happened: "the coming forth endowed you with the human birthright of your individuality."

One Serbian immigrant expressed what had taken place for so many others. He had come over in steerage, had worked in a cracker factory by day and studied by night to win a scholarship to Columbia University (where he later became a professor). After graduation from the university, he returned to Europe for further studies. He later recalled what he had said to himself as the ship pulled away from New York harbor, a personal message of pride in his dual identity as a hyphenated American. He celebrated what he had brought to America and he was celebrating what he was bringing to Europe:

"Michael Pupin, the most valuable asset which you carried into New York harbor nine years ago was your knowedge of, and respect and admiration for, the best traditions of your race . . . the most valuable asset which you are now taking with you from New York harbor is your knowledge of, and profound respect and admiration for, the best traditions of your adopted country."

116

9 THE WISH TO REMEMBER

*The taste will be
forever in his mouth*

I began this immigrant retrospective at the Golden Door of Ellis Island where millions of immigrants entered the United States.

I end it with a visit to Ellis Island some 356 years after the *Mayflower* landed on the Massachusetts coast with 102 immigrants, more than 200 years after the birth of the United States, and approximately 64 years after my own father landed.

I went back again with my father who came from Lebanon in 1912 and with my son who at fifteen was almost the same age as my father had been when he first saw Ellis Island. Both son and grandson wanted *to remember* in what has become an increasingly common reaction in America. Historian Marcus Hansen observed that "what the son wishes to forget the grandson wishes to remember." He has proved only partly accurate. Today, both wish to remember.

As the three of us walked toward the main building on Ellis Island, my father also remembered. With a start, he pointed to the hospital building where he had been detained a week for a physical checkup — not knowing whether he would ever get past the Golden Door.

In our group of visitors, there was another father-and-son

combination as well as a Polish tailor who compared notes with my father on his own detention at Ellis Island. At the main building, we walked through the deserted and empty baggage room which was once a noisy jumble of sacks, trunks, battered suitcases, and assorted bits and pieces of personal belongings from all over the world. We went upstairs to the giant hall and sat on the same wooden benches once used by five thousand immigrants at a time as they waited for an immigration inspector to say yes or no.

Our group, like hundreds of others who came beginning with the reopening of Ellis Island to visitors during the summer and fall of 1976, were testifying to the strong *wish to remember*:

To remember the immigrant experience.

To remember their roots in the Old Country.

To remember how different nationalities wove different biographies in America.

To remember how this country has been put together.

To remember in order to understand better ourselves and our neighbors.

To remember that time passes and we are part of its passage.

To share in what Henry James once said of a visit to Ellis Island, an observation that also applies to learning about the immigrant experience: Each of us comes back "not at all the same person that he went, he has eaten of the tree of knowledge, and the taste will be forever in his mouth."

From crowded street festivals for San Gennaro along New York's Mulberry Street to the Polish-flavored "Melody of Love" by singer Bobby Vinton, from Hellenic parades to new courses on Scandinavian languages at the University of Texas in Austin, the *wish to remember* manifests itself.

As Monsignor Geno Baroni, director of the National Center for Urban Ethnic Affairs, points out, the United States is "probably the most ethnic and culturally pluralistic country in

118

the world" and "today we are rediscovering the pluralistic character of America."

Ralph J. Perotta, executive director of the New York Center for Ethnic Affairs, went further: "If diversity was once a luxury we could not afford, now it is a reality we can no longer avoid." A Chicago Polish-American who made it to the U.S. Congress, Roman Pucinski, has cited "a quiet ethnic revolution" and "a revival of the ethnic spirit."

Appropriately, it was in America's bicentennial year, 1976, that the signs of that revival became increasingly evident. Two different magazines were launched for an estimated twenty million Italian-Americans, *I-AM* and *Identity*. The editor of the latter told potential subscribers: "I'd love to see the smiling faces, the joy and enthusiasm as you and your family discover that *at last* we've got a magazine that celebrates the Italian-American. Delizioso!"

An official of the Kosciuzko Foundation in New York reported "a great deal more interest among the young especially" in their ethnic backgrounds. Calling it "a third-generation phenomenon," he added that Polish names are being changed back to the original spelling. For example, many Kowalskis who changed to the English equivalent of Smith are changing back to Kowalski.

On the grounds of St. Joseph's Seminary in Yonkers, New York, two thousand competed in the forty-fourth annual feis of the United Irish Counties Association, reciting poems in Gaelic, delivering orations, and, particularly, dancing Irish jigs and playing Irish tunes. One Irish mother with an Italian husband and two sons who won trophies doing Irish dances said of the competitions: "Sometimes you come home with a lot of trophies, but sometimes you just come home with a headache." But that didn't stop the family, and many others, from always coming to the feis.

In Mt. Jewett, Pennsylvania, descendants of Swedish immigrants told a newspaper correspondent from Sweden of the renewed interest in Swedish culture, customs, and languages.

But "it has not always been this way," noted one Swedish-American. "When I was young there was no Swedish spoken in most Swedish-American homes. It wasn't the thing to do. As quickly as possible we were supposed to blend in, to pick up the habits and customs of the new country, the language and forms of expression."

In Chicago, 750,000 German-speaking radio listeners have their own German-language disc jockey, Gerd Sklomar, who plays records, gives the news, and delivers commercials over three different FM stations. Polish-Americans in New York had Bill Shibilski, a musical Pied Piper who started out in 1964 when there were only two polka shows on New York radio. A dozen years later there were twenty-five polka programs on fifteen different stations, part of a groundswell of ethnic programming on radio stations all over the country.

From suburbs everywhere, "Saturday ethnics" emerge. They drive their station wagons to downtown ethnic neighborhoods to buy familiar foods, spices, and pastries. In referring to Italian-Americans, journalist Nicholas Pileggi has commented that "it is only with a trunk filled with Italian market produce that a Saturday Italian can face six days in the suburbs."

In Washington, D.C., the capital celebrated the country's ethnic variety with exhibits and pavilions, as did Toronto, Canada (where the many first-generation immigrants bring to mind the U.S. "new immigration" in the early part of this century). In the single month of August, 1976, Michigan had a Polish Festival in Wyandotte; an Arab World Festival, a Polish Festival, a Scandinavian Fair, and an East Indian Festival in Detroit; and an annual Danish Festival in Greenville.

In ethnic festivals, the basic ingredients are traditional costumes, folk dances and songs, arts and crafts — and food. The shortest distance to an ethnic mind and heart is through the stomach, a route that draws in nonmembers of the group as well. When a third- or fourth-generation palate no longer waters at ethnic dishes, then assimilation has really taken place.

From all appearances, this has not happened. Not only are ethnic Americans still strongly devoted to their national dishes, they have generated interest among other groups as well. A tour of downtown restaurants in American cities constitutes an ethnic pilgrimage.

More than the palate is involved. For ethnic Americans, familiar dishes bring contact with the past, with the warmth of childhood, with family celebrations on holy days, with the childhood security feelings of being loved, treasured, and fully accepted. (Later, came the thrusting out into the cold competitive marketplace.)

For Catholics in particular, growing up in America has meant eating from an ethnic table and being loved by immigrant grandparents and parents. As late as the 1960s, according to a National Opinion Research Center (NORC) study, half of the American Catholic population were either immigrants or children of immigrants. In the 1970s, eighty percent had at least one immigrant grandparent and more than half (fifty-five percent) had all four grandparents born abroad. NORC also found that over half of American Catholics lived in neighborhoods where one-half or more of their neighbors have the same nationality. As a Polish-American stated in 1971:

> I'm Polish. I mean, I'm American. My family has been here for four generations; that's a lot. My great-grandfather came over here, from near Cracow. I've never been to Poland. I'll never go there. Why should I? It's in your blood. It's in your background. But I live here. My wife is the same, Polish. We're just like other people in this country, but we have memories, Polish memories, that's what my grandfather used to say: "John, don't let your kids forget that once upon a time the family was in Poland." How could I forget? My wife won't let me. She says you have to stay with your own people. We don't have only Polish people living near us, but there are a lot. Mostly we see my family and my wife's family on the weekends, so there's no time to spend doing anything else.

121

For Michael Novak, a Slovak Catholic who has achieved renown as a philosopher and social commentator, "identification with an ethnic group is a source of values, instincts, ideas, and perceptions that throw original light on the meaning of America." Novak, all four of whose grandparents were immigrants, decided in the 1970s to concentrate much of his energy on the Ethnic Millions Political Action Committee and to assert the importance of being ethnic.

Like many other ethnic Americans, Novak was trying to make his own identity clear — to himself and to others. This is how he explained his hyphenated identity during a conversation:

> If I go back to Slovakia, I don't fit. I'm not Slovak only. My family has not lived there for three generations and there have been enormous changes in these last three generations. In Slovakia, the cousins who are my age could not go back three generations either. There is a great gulf between me and my cousins. Yet, neither I nor my children will ever be Jewish-American or Irish-American or Italian-American or any other kind of American. We are what we are, and therefore to some extent very American — as American as anybody. Yet we're not like other Americans.
>
> So it seems to me that all who came to America do participate in common experiences and do begin to participate in a common history, but in different ways. They bring to these experiences different perceptions, different expectations, and they meet people on somewhat different terms. At one and the same time, you have a kind of unity and a very impressive diversity. That's the pattern of assimilation in the United States and it's a very complicated one.
>
> The really important question is: How capable is America of assimilating the wisdom and the perceptions brought by the immigrants? It's not only up to the immigrants to assimilate; it's also up to America to change and to be changed in order to become more like the immigrants.

As far as Novak is concerned, Catholics who loosen their ethnic identity tend to loosen their religious affiliation. It is a point worth considering, particularly in the light of the importance of faith to America's immigrants. "There is a very severe problem of faith among those Catholics who are trying to live as if they have no specific culture, as though they're American just like everybody else," Novak says. "They give up the specific identity of being Catholic, in its many variations, in favor of a secular humanism with either a radical, a conservative, or a liberal tinge. And it seems to me that they become much more 'American' than Catholic."

For those ethnic Americans who are becoming more aware of their immigrant roots, a celebration is taking place. They are celebrating who they are by coming to terms with where they came from and how the immigrant process shaped them. It is more than coming to terms. It is building self-esteem by learning to esteem their own backgrounds.

One part of the process is the realization of how hard *all* immigrant groups had it. Just changing overnight from familiar to strange ways was a shock that threatened to undermine every immigrant. They soon realized that America was not enthusiastically welcoming every aspect of them. It was primarily their manpower and womanpower that was being welcomed — not their "alien" ways. They quickly learned what comedian Sam Levenson said his father discovered when he came over from the Old Country: (1) that the streets were not paved with gold, (2) that most of the streets were not even paved, and (3) that he had to help pave them.

The immigrants literally paved the way for their children and their children's children. It was at great personal expense. Uprooted, overworked, and overwhelmed by their strange new world, they went about sinking the new roots to which succeeding generations are linked. Whether or not ethnic groups are "unmeltable," as Novak argues, most Americans are so close to their immigrant origins that they cannot understand themselves and those around them without taking into account the immigrant experience.

The immigrants knew where they came from; they struggled to find out where they had come. Their children, grandchildren, and great-grandchildren may know where they are, but they face the effort of learning about where they came from. The past shapes the present and influences the future. To know our parents and grandparents is to know their history as immigrants. Not to know of that experience is to remain to some degree uprooted. To search for identity — a task facing everyone — requires a search for roots, both old and new.

That is the wisdom of the young grandchildren of immigrants — the third generation that historian Hansen says wishes to remember. They want to touch the past to get a sense of security and to develop their burgeoning identity. When young, they love to touch the family past in the arms of grandparents. When growing up, they want to touch the historical past, too. When grown up, that sense of touch is not only comforting and reassuring, it is part of the sense of self.

That is why my son and I wanted to revisit Ellis Island, why it has been important to visit the Old Country, and why it has been important to listen to the past — a past nourished by faith and sustained by hope. Each of us, in the nation of immigrants, is linked to that immigrant experience of faith and hope. It is our living legacy.

SELECTED BIBLIOGRAPHY

Immigrant Experience in General

Stanley Feldstein and Lawrence Costello (eds.), *The Ordeal of Assimilation* (Anchor Books, 1974).

Nathan Glazer and Daniel Patrick Moynihan, *Beyond the Melting Pot* (M.I.T. Press, 1963).

Oscar Handlin, *The Uprooted* (Grosset & Dunlap, 1951).

———— (ed.), *Immigration As a Factor in American History* (Prentice-Hall, 1959).

John Higham, *Strangers in the Land* (Atheneum, 1969).

Ann Novotny, *Strangers at the Door* (Bantam Books, 1971).

Thomas C. Wheeler (ed.), *The Immigrant Experience* (Dial Press, 1971).

Carl Wittke, *We Who Built America* (Case Western Reserve University Press, rev. ed. 1967).

The Irish

Stephen Birmingham, *Real Lace* (Harper & Row, 1973).

Andrew M. Greeley, *That Most Distressful Nation* (Quadrangle Books, 1972).

George Potter, *To the Golden Door: The Story of the Irish in Ireland and America* (Little, Brown & Co., 1960).

Oscar Handlin, *Boston's Immigrants* (Atheneum, 1970).

William V. Shannon, *The American Irish* (Macmillan, rev. ed. 1966).

Edward Wakin, *Enter the Irish-American* (Thomas Y. Crowell Co., 1976).

Carl Wittke, *The Irish in America* (Louisiana State University Press, 1956).

The Germans

Dieter Cunz, *They Came from Germany* (Dodd, Mead, 1966).

Theodore Huebener, *The Germans in America* (Chilton Company, 1962).

Richard O'Connor, *The German-Americans* (Little, Brown & Co., 1968).

LaVern Rippley, *Of German Ways* (Dillon Press, 1970).

Carl Wittke, *Refugees of Revolution: The German Forty-Eighters in America* (Greenwood Press, 1952).

The Scandinavians

Adolph B. Benson and Naboth Hedin (eds.), *Swedes in America* (Haskell House, 1969).

Kendric C. Babock, *The Scandinavian Element in the United States* (1914), (Arno Press, 1969).

Donald S. Connery, *The Scandinavians* (Eyre & Spottiswoode, 1966).

Vilhelm Moberg, *Unto A Good Land* (Popular Library, 1973, a novel originally published in 1954).

O. E. Rolvaag, *Giants in the Earth* (Harper & Brothers, 1927). A novel.

Olak Morgan Norlie, *History of the Norwegian People in America* (Augsburg Publishing House, 1925).

The Italians

Alexander DeConde, *Half Bitter, Half Sweet* (Scribner's, 1972).

Richard Gambino, *Blood of My Blood* (Doubleday & Co., 1974).

Joseph Lopreato, *Italian Americans* (Random House, 1970).

Wayne Moquin (ed.), *A Documentary History of the Italian Americans* (Praeger, 1974).

Lawrence F. Pisani, *The Italian in America* (Exposition Press, 1957).

The Poles

Paul Fox, *The Poles in America* (George H. Doranx Co., 1922).

Arthur Evans Wood, *Hamtramck Then and Now* (Bookman Associates, 1955).

Joseph A. Wytrwal, *America's Polish Heritage* (Endurance Press, 1961).

————, *Poles in American History and Tradition* (Endurance Press, 1969).

The Jews

Nathan Glazer, *American Judaism* (University of Chicago Press, 1957).

Isaac Metzker (ed.), *A Bintel Brief* (Ballantine Books, 1971).

Marshall Sklare, *America's Jews* (Random House, 1971).

———— (ed.), *The Jews: Social Patterns of An American Group* (Free Press, 1958).

Judd L. Teller, *Strangers and Natives* (Delacorte Press, 1968).

INDEX

129